The New Jersey
COASTAL
HERITAGE TRAIL

A Top-to-Bottom Tour of More Than
50 Scenic and Historic Sites

Patricia Robinson

Plexus Publishing, Inc.
Medford, New Jersey

First Printing, 2007

The New Jersey Coastal Heritage Trail: A Top-to-Bottom Tour of More Than 50 Scenic and Historic Sites

Copyright © 2007 by Patricia Robinson

Published by: Plexus Publishing, Inc.
                  143 Old Marlton Pike
                  Medford, NJ 08055

Library of Congress Cataloging-in-Publication Data

Robinson, Patricia (Patricia Claire)
  The New Jersey Coastal Heritage Trail : a top-to-bottom tour of more than 50 scenic and historic sites / Patricia Robinson.
       p. cm.
  Includes bibliographical references and index.
    ISBN 978-0-937548-58-5
  1. New Jersey Coastal Heritage Trail (N.J.)--Tours. 2. New Jersey--History, Local--Guidebooks. 3. Historic sites--New Jersey--Guidebooks. 4. Landscape--New Jersey--Guidebooks. I. Title.
   F142.N48R63 2007
    917.4904'44—dc22

                                                                2006037415

Printed and bound in China.

President and CEO: Thomas H. Hogan, Sr.
Editor-in-Chief and Publisher: John B. Bryans
Managing Editor: Amy M. Reeve
VP Graphics and Production: M. Heide Dengler
Book Designer: Kara Jalkowski
Cover Designer: Michele Quinn
Sales Manager: Pat Palatucci
Copyeditor: Pat Hadley-Miller
Proofreader: Lisa Schaad
Indexer: Beth Palmer

For Anne, Charlie, Sandy,
Chris, Nicky, and Jake,
who, for their various reasons,
love the Jersey Shore

Contents

Part 1: Sandy Hook Region

Part 2: Barnegat Bay Region

Part 3: Absecon and Cape May Regions

Part 4: Delsea Region

Acknowledgments

You can't produce a book about such an extensive subject like the New Jersey Coastal Heritage Trail without the help, support, and direction of a cast of thousands.

First, my deepest and profound thanks to Governor Thomas Kean, on whose watch this trail was created, for taking the time to write this book's Foreword. Because of his tenures as state governor and president of Drew University, not to mention his role in other affairs of state, the world has been made a better place.

Thanks to Philip Correll, project director of the New Jersey Coastal Heritage Trail, who wholeheartedly endorsed this idea from its inception, and who was the first to point me in the right direction in my initial fact-finding stage.

Thanks also to the following:

To Bob Allen, director of Conservation Science at the Nature Conservancy, for his help when I visited the Eldora Nature Preserve; Mary Bean, the Tuckerton Seaport docent who shared the back-story about "Ralph"; Alicia Bjornson, who so graciously spent her time discussing the Hancock House State Historic Site one freezing, February morning; Kathy Dwyer of the Twin Lights State Historic Site; and James Faczak, resource interpretive specialist at Cheesequake State Park.

To Heidi Hanlon at the Cape May National Wildlife Refuge in Cape May Court House; Beth Huch, supervisor of education and interpretation at Tuckerton Seaport; Rich Isaacson of the Belford Seafood Co-Op, who opened my eyes to the harsh realities of the modern fisherman; dispatcher Fran Johnson of the Lacey Township Police Department, who provided the "right" directions to Double Trouble State Park when I got in trouble and lost my way; "Cap'n" Fred Kalm, skipper of the *Melody II*, Tuckerton Seaport; and Bob Marshall of the Aeolium Nature Center, Island Beach State Park.

To Lorraine McCay, resource interpretive specialist, Allaire State Park; Chris and Gordon Miller, two gregarious equestrians I met on the beach bridle path at Island Beach State Park one glorious October morning; Steve Murray, superintendent of parks for the City of North Wildwood, who gave me a fantastic tour of the Hereford Inlet Lighthouse; Patricia Perrini, recreation leader, Cattus Island County Park; Lyle Richards, lighthouse docent, Tuckerton Seaport; Terry Colleen Terry, Tuckahoe Wildlife Management Area; and Joe Walton, master decoy carver, Tuckerton Seaport.

To Carole Grabowski and Catherine and Robert Moore of the Keyport Historical Society, who regaled me with many stories during my visit to the Steamboat Dock Museum.

To the crews of the U.S. Coast Guard stations at Barnegat Bay and Atlantic City, who were gracious to take me on impromptu tours. Stay safe, guys and gals.

To the volunteers and crew of the *A. J. Meerwald*, who warmly tolerated the crazy photographer skittering around their busy deck.

To Judi Raimos and Alex Zupko at Bernardsville One-Hour Photo and the lab technicians at Park Lane, Chatham, who were invaluable in preparing the photos used in this book; and to the staff of Universal Photo Supplies, Lakewood, for keeping me well-supplied with film, especially when I needed it at the last minute. (An aside: Most of the photos in this book were shot with Canon 35-mm SLR film equipment using Fuji Provia 100F slide film and Canon digital SLRs.)

And, of course, thanks to everyone at Plexus Publishing, Inc., the true force behind this book: To president and CEO Tom Hogan, Sr., for believing in the project; to my editor and publisher, John Bryans, who jump-started this project with a simple, "let's do another book"; to my managing editor, Amy Reeve, for moving this book through the pipeline; and to Plexus's sales manager and chief cook and bottle washer, Pat Palatucci, to whom I may still owe a few margaritas.

Last but not least, a big thanks to the employees of every Wawa convenience store I visited between Barnegat Bay and Fort Mott. With apologies to Napoleon, writers, like soldiers, march on their stomachs, and every single Wawa I visited served me very, very well. By the way, in case you didn't know, "Wawa" is how the Lenni-Lenape referred to the Canada goose.

Patricia Robinson

Foreword

During my term as governor of New Jersey, I was fortunate to be able to travel our great state every day. New Jersey is blessed with a great wealth and variety of historic and beautiful locations. Not least among these are the locations that comprise the New Jersey Coastal Heritage Trail. Created by an act of Congress in 1988, the Coastal Heritage Trail provides for "public appreciation, education, understanding, and enjoyment of significant natural and cultural sites associated with the coastal area of the State of New Jersey."

Pat Robinson's book, *The New Jersey Coastal Heritage Trail: A Top-to-Bottom Tour of More Than 50 Scenic and Historic Sites,* provides an excellent overview of the trail as well as detailed information about the many sites and historical happenings up and down the Atlantic and Delaware River coasts of New Jersey. With Pat's help, readers can relive New Jersey's own colonial tea party in Greenwich, track the seasonal migration of birds in Cape May, or immerse themselves in the storied history of the Navesink Twin Lights.

This comprehensive guide will surely be a treasured resource for those who hope to discover—or rediscover—all that New Jersey has to offer.

—Thomas H. Kean

How to Use This Book

To make it easy for visitors to get around, the state of New Jersey divided the Coastal Heritage Trail into five regions: Sandy Hook, Barnegat Bay, Absecon, Cape May, and Delsea. Attractions in these regions, in turn, were grouped into "themes," including Wildlife Migration (e.g., Cape May Point State Park and Edwin B. Forsythe National Wildlife Refuge); Coastal Habitats (e.g., Cattus Island County Park and Island Beach State Park); and Maritime History (e.g., Tuckerton Seaport and Bayshore Discovery Project). As this book goes to press, additional themes, "Relaxation and Inspiration" and "Historic Settlements," are still under development.

In writing this book, I have taken my cue from the official trail maps and presented my material by region. The regions appear in separate sections, with the exception of the Absecon and Cape May regions: These regions are combined into one section as they are in the state's official trail documentation.

I further treat the regions as one consecutive trail, starting in the east "at the top" with the Perth Amboy Harbor Walk in the Sandy Hook region, and proceeding clockwise to Fort Mott State Park.

For the sake of simplicity, however, I have refrained from identifying venues by theme, since one venue can fit into two or more themes.

A summary of the regions and their attractions follows.

SANDY HOOK REGION

The Sandy Hook Region extends along Raritan Bay from Perth Amboy, at the tip of Raritan Bay, south to the border of Monmouth and Ocean counties along the Atlantic Ocean. Sites and activities include:

Perth Amboy Harbor Walk
Steamboat Dock Museum
Belford Seafood Co-Op
Leonardo State Marina
Mount Mitchill Scenic Overlook
Twin Lights State Historic Site
Sandy Hook Unit of the Gateway National Recreation Area
Cheesequake State Park
Allaire State Park

BARNEGAT BAY REGION

The Barnegat Bay Region extends from the Monmouth County and Ocean County border in the north to Great Bay, south of Little Egg Harbor. Sites include:

Cattus Island County Park
Toms River Seaport Society Maritime Museum
Island Beach State Park
Double Trouble State Park
Forked River State Marina
Eno's Pond County Park
Barnegat Lighthouse State Park
U.S. Coast Guard Station, Barnegat Light
Tuckerton Seaport
Great Bay Boulevard Wildlife Management Area

ABSECON AND CAPE MAY REGIONS

Because of its brevity, the Absecon Region is combined with the Cape May Region. As one, the area extends from Great Bay south to Cape May County, south of Green Creek. Sites of interest include:

Edwin B. Forsythe National Wildlife Refuge
U.S. Coast Guard Station, Atlantic City

Sen. Frank S. Farley State Marina
Tuckahoe Wildlife Management Area
Corson's Inlet State Park
The Wetlands Institute
Hereford Inlet Lighthouse
Cape May Migratory Bird Refuge
Cape May Point State Park
Higbee Beach Wildlife Management Area

DELSEA REGION

The most extensive region on the trail, the Delsea region extends from Cape May Court House in the south up the Delaware Bay to Fort Mott State Park outside of Pennsville at the southern end of the New Jersey Turnpike. Trail sites include:

Cape May National Wildlife Refuge
Cape May Bird Observatory
Dennis Creek Wildlife Management Area
Belleplain State Forest
Eldora Nature Preserve
Dennis Township Wetland Restoration Site
Maurice River Township Wetland Restoration Site
East Point Lighthouse
Heislerville Wildlife Management Area
Bayshore Discovery Project
Commercial Township Wetland Restoration Site
Egg Island Wildlife Management Area
Glades Wildlife Refuge
Fortescue State Marina
Peaslee Wildlife Management Area
Manumuskin River Preserve
Peek Preserve
Green Swamp Nature Area
Greenwich Tea Burning Monument
Stow Creek Viewing Area
Hancock House State Historic Site

Alloway Creek Watershed Wetland Restoration Site
Finn's Point Rear Range Light
Finn's Point National Cemetery
Fort Mott State Park

A WORD ABOUT TRAIL CHANGES

Because the trail is a "work in progress," there are some changes to information in this book that may differ from older, official documentation.

The Barnegat Bay Decoy and Baymen's Museum listed on the state's official map for the Barnegat Bay Region has now been incorporated into Tuckerton Seaport, and its location has moved from Tip Seaman Park to the seaport across the street.

The Delsea Region's Delaware Bay Schooner Project is now the Bayshore Discovery Center.

Finally, the directions to Double Trouble State Park in the Barnegat Bay Region have changed, thanks to a reconfiguration of exits along the Garden State Parkway.

A word about fees: Many of these venues, like the Perth Amboy Harbor Walk and Cape May National Wildlife Refuge, are free, while others, like the Hancock House State Historic Site and Hereford Inlet Lighthouse, suggest a small donation. Still others, notably the larger state parks like Island Beach, Cheesequake, and Allaire, have set seasonal fees.

Some sites, especially the wildlife management areas, may also be closed during certain hunting seasons throughout the fall into spring, so you may want to call ahead of time. Some hunting is also allowed at the Edwin B. Forsythe National Wildlife Refuge and some wetland restoration sites. The state, however, prohibits hunting on Sunday.

Please be aware that trail descriptions are likely to change over time. When visiting a trail, always try to obtain the most up-to-date guide at the facility.

A WORD ABOUT ENTRY LENGTHS

Descriptions for some entries in this book, like those for Belleplain State Forest and Island Beach State Park, are lengthier than those for, say, Fortescue State Marina or Stow Creek Viewing Area.

There's a practical reason for this. Some destinations simply offer a wider range of things for visitors to see and do. Big or small, every entry in this book is a true Jersey gem.

Entries are numbered—for example, the Perth Amboy Harbor Walk is "1," Steamboat Dock Museum, "2," and so on. If an entry is referenced in another entry, it will be indicated by [see #1], [see #2], etc.

SPECIFIC INTERESTS AND ACTIVITIES

Want to know where specific interests and activities, like bird-watching, lighthouses, or photography, can be found on the New Jersey Coastal Heritage Trail? Appendix A lists sites according to interest.

SOME CAUTIONS

Nature and wildlife cannot be controlled. Coastal downpours explode from nowhere. Snakes will bask on a trail when the weather is warm.

Wear appropriate clothing and hiking boots. Use suntan lotion and insect repellent when necessary. In winter, if you expect to tackle an icy path, bring crampons. At all times, carry water and something to nibble.

Remember, New Jersey's unofficial insects are the deer tick and the mosquito. You may want to wear a hat and long-sleeved shirt, and it's a good idea to tuck your pants into your socks.

Have a great time!

Introduction
Exploring New Jersey's Best-Kept Secret

Sail a tall ship, bike a barrier island, paddle a pirate's cove ... and never leave New Jersey.

These are just a few of the adventures awaiting explorers on the New Jersey Coastal Heritage Trail, the state's best-kept, albeit publicized, secret.

Strange but true, despite the brochures and signage produced to lure visitors to the Trail, few people know it exists. Yet the 275-mile trail, created by an act of Congress in 1988 to, as the state brochures say, "provide for public understanding and enjoyment of sites and resources associated with the coastal area," harbors some of the state's best natural and historical gems, many of them free for the visiting.

The Trail also offers some wonderful trivia. For example:

- The Lenni-Lenape Indians, Jersey's original tenants, used the dark purple part of clamshells for their money, or "wampum."

- Confederate soldiers are buried in Finn's Point National Cemetery along the Delaware Bay.

- New Jersey's official tall ship is a 20th-century oyster schooner, the *A. J. Meerwald.*

- The Jersey version of the Boston Tea Party was held in the tiny village of Greenwich in Cumberland County in 1774.

I'll be serious now. To know where you're going, you have to know where you're coming from. Briefly, here is what you'll learn on the New Jersey Coastal Heritage Trail.

LOCAL TOURISM

The Jersey coast, with its sandy beaches and fertile coastal plains, has always attracted visitors. The Lenni-Lenape Indians used Atlantic Ocean barrier islands, such as Sandy Hook, for summer hunting grounds long before they were "discovered" by 16th-century European explorers the likes of Henry Hudson. By the late 19th-century, beach communities, like those at Cape May and Barnegat Bay, provided cool refuge for city dwellers anxious to escape the stifling heat of New York and Philadelphia. This tradition continues.

MILITARY HISTORY

During the Revolutionary War, local coves and estuaries provided sanctuary for colonial privateers, who attacked British ships for supplies they shared with the Continental Army. Sandy Hook lighthouse exchanged hands between Colonial and British forces several times, while the Hancock House outside Salem was the scene of a grisly massacre of colonial militia by British troops.

Since lower New Jersey is a peninsula, both coasts provided excellent settings for military forts. Sandy Hook's Fort Hancock was initially built to protect New York Harbor. Fort Mott State Park was part of a three-fort defense system initially created to protect Philadelphia and other ports along the Delaware Bay and River.

LOCAL INDUSTRIES

On a more peaceful note, several indigenous industries evolved over the centuries. Allaire Village at Allaire State Park was a 19th-century forge town. The lumber/farm company town at Double Trouble State Park, which thrived in the early- to mid-20th century, relied on two native industries, the milling of Atlantic white cedar, and harvesting of cranberry bogs.

The coastal waters spawned their own industries and cultures. Throughout the 19th and 20th centuries, Bivalve, the home of the Discovery Bayshore Project, boasted one of the state's largest oyster harvesting and processing operations. Tuckerton and surrounding communities throughout the Barnegat Bay area enjoyed a vibrant commercial fishing industry.

New Jersey was also birthplace to the precursor of the U.S. Coast Guard—the U.S. Life-Saving Service, created in 1848 by a Toms River resident to aid the survivors of ships that had wrecked among the shoals and currents of the treacherous coast. Existing lighthouses were also among the first in the mid-19th century to be equipped with Fresnel lenses, large lamps with primed glass that enabled their lights to be seen by ships miles out to sea.

NATURAL OFFERINGS

The state's location along the Atlantic migration corridor makes it, every spring and fall, the perfect migration motel for thousands of birds, butterflies, and aquatic mammals. Cape May is one of the most popular birding spots in the world, as is the Edwin B. Forsythe National Wildlife Refuge in Oceanville, on the outskirts of Atlantic City.

There are also many beautiful natural habitats one can find along the Trail. Cheesequake State Park is home to an Atlantic white cedar forest whose trees are more than 150 years old. Manumuskin River Preserve and the Eldora Nature Preserve are home to various rare plants and moth species. Island Beach State Park harbors what is among the state's last examples of pristine barrier island ecosystems.

Want to learn more? Read on ....

Ogle a skyline ... play in the surf ... watch the hawks fly ...

Part 1
Sandy Hook Region

Perth Amboy Harbor Walk
Bayside History Lesson

OVERVIEW

Poised at the mouth of the Arthur Kill and the top of Raritan Bay, Perth Amboy played an important part in the early history of New Jersey and the United States. Today, visitors to the city's mile-long Harbor Walk are treated to a delightful, bayside promenade that teaches as much as it entertains.

HISTORY

Founded in 1683, Perth Amboy was originally the capital of East Jersey province. When East and West Jersey merged in 1704, Perth Amboy became home to the state governor. One of those early governors was Benjamin Franklin's illegitimate son, William, who served from 1763 to 1776. During the Revolution the younger Franklin, who was a Loyalist, was taken captive by Continental troops and hustled to Connecticut, where he remained until the end of the war.

In fact, it was from Perth Amboy that, on September 11, 1776, Benjamin Franklin, along with fellow Continental Congressmen John Adams of Massachusetts and Edward Rutledge of South Carolina, embarked to Staten Island to parlay with British Admiral Richard Howe.

Perth Amboy Harbor Walk
Waterfront, City of Perth Amboy
Middlesex County
Phone: (732) 442-6421

Hours: Harbor Walk is open daily from dawn to dusk. The Perth Amboy Historical Association conducts tours of the Kearny Cottage each Tuesday and Thursday; for more information, call the Association at (732) 826-1826.

Directions:
From the North: Take Route 287 south to State Highway 440 east to the State Street exit. Continue on that street until it intersects with Lewis Street. Turn right on Lewis Street, proceed for one block, and turn left on Catalpa Street. Stay on Catalpa until you reach the waterfront.

From the West: Take the New Jersey Turnpike to Exit 10 and follow signs to Route 440. Follow above directions from State Street exit.

From the South: Take either Route 35 north into Perth Amboy to State Street and turn left on Lewis to Catalpa, or proceed up Route 9 north to 440 and follow the above directions from State Street exit.

Throughout the 19th century the city was an important commercial center for the burgeoning New York metropolitan area. But, like many other Garden State cities, Perth Amboy suffered its economic ups and downs in the 20th century. A restoration project in the 1980s, which included the Harbor Walk, has added considerably to the city's charm.

On the path of the Perth Amboy Harbor Walk ➤

TRAIL

The walk is easy and enjoyable, especially in early morning, as the city yawns itself awake and the sun casts a warm, golden glow over the water. Egrets wade on the shoreline and seagulls' cries fill the air. Concealed in the mist, their holds bulging with cargo, ships creep north toward the Outerbridge Crossing, the steel vein that connects New Jersey and New York.

Start at Harbor Walk's southern side on Front Street. At Catalpa Street, turn left and proceed uphill to a small, yellow clapboard house. This is the Kearny Cottage, built in 1781 by the affluent Kearny family.

Return to the harbor and continue walking northward, past the Veterans Memorial that was installed in 2005. The white gazebo on your left is particularly pretty in summer, when its garden is lush with day lilies and assorted wildflowers.

As you continue on, you'll see a sign that calls your attention to a small white bump sitting off Ward's Point on Staten Island. This is the 61-foot-tall

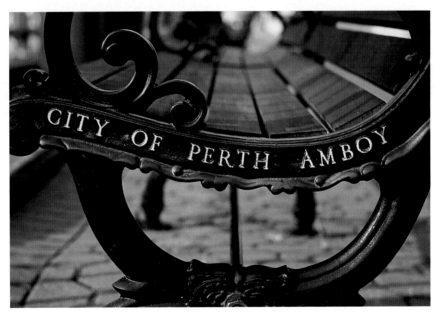

Bench on the path of the Perth Amboy Harbor Walk

◀ *Raritan Yacht Club*

Great Beds Light. Operated by the U.S. Coast Guard, the light has been in continuous operation since it was built in 1880.

Another sign draws your attention to the wooded cliffs across the bay: the Bluffs, where Franklin, Adams, and Rutledge had that parlay with Howe. There's an interesting aside to their excursion. To ensure the safety of the Congressmen, Howe dispatched an officer to Perth Amboy to serve as a hostage. But Franklin, Adams, and Rutledge so trusted Howe that they brought the officer with them.

The large white house sitting on a hill is the Raritan Yacht Club, or, as its red letters tout, the RYC. The club, which offers more than 200 moorings for boaters, is one of the oldest in the country and the oldest in the state. It was founded in 1882 with the merger of the Carteret Yacht Club (1865) and the Perth Amboy Yacht Club (1874).

The next attraction on the trail is the municipal marina. On any given morning, the harbor's municipal parking lot is a bustle of activity. Local fishermen come to try their luck angling off the long, narrow docks. Joggers stretch their limbs preparing for a post-dawn jog.

To the left of the marina is a restaurant with the martial moniker of Seabra's Armory. Built in 1930, the three-story, neo-Georgian brick building was once the Perth Amboy Naval Militia Armory, housing offices, classrooms, a rifle range, and drill hall. Abandoned in the 1960s, the building was turned into a restaurant and banquet facility in 1985. Take a look at the top of its Front Street façade: Etched into the stone is the militia's coat of arms.

Following the trail to the left will take you to the next point of historic interest, the Tottenville ferry building. Listed on the National Historic Register, the small wooden structure was once the terminal for ferry service between Perth Amboy and Tottenville, New York. Today, pleasure boats leave from its wharves.

TRIVIA

Perth Amboy got its name in a roundabout way. The Lenni-Lenape Indians, from whom the land was purchased, called it Ompoge. In time this name mutated to Amboyle and, finally, to Amboy. "Perth" was added to honor the English Earl of Perth, one of the proprietors who managed the area under a Royal grant.

2

Steamboat Dock Museum
Rum Runners and Cavalry Boots

OVERVIEW

Set on a series of rolling hills backdropped by Raritan Bay, Keyport, a historic and charming little town, offers visitors a chance to grab a bite, visit its many parks, or simply enjoy the waterfront view. Its history can be enjoyed at the charming and quaint, not to mention memorabilia-laden, Steamboat Dock Museum. Here visitors can see exhibits about the town's former primary industries: oystering and steamboat and seaplane building.

The museum, owned by the Keyport Historical Society and operated since 1976, is a charming destination on its own, although many visitors will stop here when going to or coming from the Sandy Hook Unit of the Gateway National Recreation Area [see #7]. But take note: This little delight is only open at specific times mid-May through September, so call ahead. Tours can also be arranged by appointment.

HISTORY

The tiny, single-story building in which the museum is housed once belonged to the Keansburg Steamboat Company. Steamboats were manufactured in Keyport from 1840 to 1870, and typically launched from here—hence, the name Steamboat Dock. According to museum docents, sailors from the

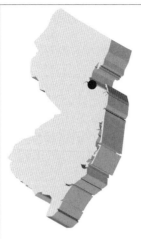

Steamboat Dock Museum
Broad Street and American Legion Drive
Keyport, Monmouth County
Phone: (732) 739-6390

Hours: Seasonal (Mid-May or June–September), 1 P.M. to 4 P.M. Sunday; 10 A.M. to 2 P.M. Monday
Fees: None, but a donation is suggested
Facilities: Interpretive exhibits, gift shop, and restrooms

Directions:
From the North: Take the Garden State Parkway to Exit 117; take Route 36 east to the Broad Street jughandle, and proceed down Broad Street. Broad Street intersects with American Legion Drive at the waterfront. The museum is on your left.

From the West: Take the New Jersey Turnpike to Exit 10 and follow the signs to the Garden State Parkway. Take the Parkway south to Exit 117 and follow the directions above.

From the South: Take Route 36 north to Broad Street and turn right. From there, follow the directions above.

local steamboat company would often stumble into the building after a night of hard drinking and sleep right on the hardwood floor.

Keyport was also home to Aeromarine Plane and Motor. The company built seaplanes here from 1917 to 1937 and was the first to offer regular commercial airline service via its seaplanes. The planes, which flew at the astounding speed of 80 miles per hour, traveled two routes: one between Cleveland and Detroit and the other between Key West and Havana. In the heyday of the

Fish sign at the Steamboat Dock Museum

Prohibition era, the 18-passenger planes flew customers to Havana, where they could enjoy their gin while gambling in the casinos. At the same time, flights returning from Cuba would be loaded with rum. An electric engine starter and metal-clad seaplane are on exhibit at the museum.

Established in 1830, the town of Keyport itself is, for New Jersey, a relatively new community. It was originally part of one of two plantations owned by the Kearny family—the same family who owned the Kearny Cottage in Perth Amboy—who settled in the area in the early 18th century. The Kearny family was one of the area's wealthier families, owning 70 slaves and two sloops. Farm equipment, two doors, a fireplace mantle, and the deed from the plantation can all be found at the museum.

One of the more formidable displays at the museum—in fact, it has its own room—is that of the *Keyport Weekly News*, the town's early newspaper. An editor's desk and old printing press circa late 19th century are displayed, as is the large black-and-gold sign from the original newspaper office building. Several

Raritan Bay in early morning

old manual typewriters, including one from the 1880s, are also encased in a glass display.

Other displays include World War I uniforms, complete with a set of officer's cavalry boots from 1917; antique helmets from the local fire company; souvenir mugs from various Keyport celebrations; Lenni-Lenape artifacts, including a tobacco pipe made from a turtle shell; and a 1915 commemorative plating marking the completion of the Panama Canal.

While in Keyport you'll want to visit the Keyport Fire Museum at 86 Broad Street. It is the only fire museum in Monmouth County. Its many exhibits include 19th-century fire equipment; a piece of the *Hindenberg*, the German zeppelin that burned while attempting to moor at Lakehurst in 1937; and a section of steel from the World Trade Center.

TRIVIA

According to Keyport historians, most of the seaplane pilots were women. Apparently they could tolerate the cold conditions of the open cockpits better than their male counterparts.

3

Belford Seafood Co-Op
Time-Honored Heritage

OVERVIEW

Nestled alongside Compton's Creek, in a gorgeous, broad green swatch of wildlife-rich tidal marshes, the Belford Seafood Co-Op may take some doing to reach, but it's definitely worth the trip. Pirates Cove, the Co-Op's public restaurant, serves the same fresh, tasty catches that Co-Op fishermen daily send to New York's celebrated Fulton Fish Market, and to markets as far away as Philadelphia. Fresh catches can also be purchased at the Co-Op's retail store, adjacent to the restaurant.

A trip to the Co-Op is an eye-opener into the rugged life of the local fishermen. Tethered to the Co-Op wharves, waiting for the next trip down Raritan Bay out to the Atlantic, the tiny fishing boats, with their cramped quarters and weather-beaten decks, speak volumes about the fishermen's heritage.

Fishing is one of the roughest, toughest jobs in the world. As you sit in your cozy kitchen breading that flounder, or at your favorite restaurant preparing to dive into the scampi, thank the fishermen—and women—for all they do to keep us landlubbers fed and happy. Better yet, visit the Belford Seafood Co-Op and say "thank you" in person.

Belford Seafood Co-Op
901 Port Monmouth Road, Belford, NJ 07718
Monmouth County
Phone: (732) 787-6509

Hours: The retail store is open from 8:30 A.M. to 4:30 P.M. Monday through Saturday, and 8:30 A.M. to noon on Sunday. Hours for Pirates Cove Restaurant vary, so call ahead.

Directions:
From the North: Take the Garden State Parkway to Exit 117 and follow Route 36 east to Main Street in Port Monmouth. Continue on Main Street to Port Monmouth Road. Make a right. Follow the road to the Co-Op.

From the Southwest: Take the New Jersey Turnpike to Exit 10 and follow signs to the Garden State Parkway. Proceed south on the Parkway to Exit 117. From there, follow directions above.

From the Southeast: Follow Route 36 north to Main Street in Port Monmouth, then follow directions above.

HISTORY

The Co-Op opened in 1952 in an effort to bolster family businesses whose livelihoods were threatened by larger fishing operations. Today many of its members—and they number approximately 30—hail from generations of fishermen.

TRAILS

The Co-Op's bustle and noise is a jarring contrast to the peaceful marshes, where you can see egrets and herons and a goodly number of gulls and plovers.

There are no formal trails, but visitors can park near the restaurant and walk or bicycle down Port Monmouth Road. Take care: Overgrowth is high, making it difficult to see around corners.

TRIVIA

More than 200 years old, the town of Belford is considered to be the oldest working fishing port on the East Coast.

◄ *Fishing vessels at the Belford Seafood Co-Op*

4

Leonardo State Marina
A Raritan "Runway"

OVERVIEW

Located on the Raritan Bay, the Leonardo State Marina is a public put-in and mooring point for recreational boaters. This is a great place to launch for a fun ride into the bay or, if desirable, a cruise under the Verrazano Narrows Bridge into New York Harbor.

Don't have a boat? The marina still makes a fun stop. Early mornings buzz with activity as motorists stack up at the launch ramp like planes queued for take off at Newark Liberty International Airport. Photographers can get some nice dawn shots here.

The marina's operation falls under the auspices of the state Department of Environmental Protection. In recent years the state upgraded the site, adding a safety fence along Concord Avenue, landscaping, and a new picnic area, and making improvements to the parking lot.

TRIVIA

Despite the light-hearted bustle there is the stark reminder of the September 11, 2001, terrorist attacks on New York's World Trade Center.

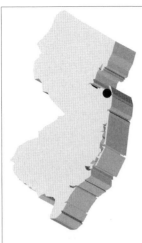

Leonardo State Marina
101 Concord Avenue
Leonardo, NJ 07737 (Mailing Address)
Monmouth County
Phone: (732) 793-0506

Hours: The Marina office is open year-round from 8 A.M. to 4 P.M.

Facilities: 179 slips that can accommodate boats up to 45 feet long; fueling station, bait and tackle shop, and restrooms

Directions:

From the North: Take the Garden State Parkway south to Exit 117 and follow Route 36 south to Leonardo. Take the Leonardo Avenue exit and continue to Center Avenue. Turn left and proceed onto Concord Avenue. Turn right. The marina will be directly on your right. Alternate route: Take the New Jersey Turnpike south to Exit 10, and follow signs to the Garden State Parkway and follow directions above.

From the West: Take the Turnpike to Exit 10, follow signs to the Garden State Parkway, and follow directions above.

From the Southeast: Follow Route 36 north into Leonardo and follow directions above.

Straight across the bay waters is the scarred skyline of lower Manhattan, void of the Twin Towers. A makeshift memorial to the tragedy stands next to the marina.

Slips at the Leonardo State Marina

5

Mount Mitchill Scenic Overlook
Aerie with an Eyeful

OVERVIEW

Rising more than 266 feet above sea level in the Atlantic Highlands, the Mount Mitchill Scenic Overlook certainly lives up to its reputation.

Want to see where you really are? The view from this spot offers a truly fantastic, bird's-eye view of the entire Raritan Bay area, encompassing the Sandy Hook Unit of the Gateway National Recreation Area [see #7] and parts of Manhattan and Long Island, New York. On a good day, you can make out the Sandy Hook Lighthouse, the control tower at John F. Kennedy International Airport on Long Island, the parachute drop at Coney Island in Brooklyn, and the Empire State Building in Manhattan.

A memorial walkway is dedicated to county residents who lost their lives in the September 11, 2001, terrorist attacks on the World Trade Center. The walkway contains plaques marking the timeline of that disastrous morning, the events of which could be seen clearly and agonizingly from here.

HISTORY

The overlook has been part of the Monmouth County Park system since 1973. It was named for Samuel Latham Mitchill (1764–1831), a physician, naturalist, and U.S. Congressman. He also helped measure the Highlands in 1816.

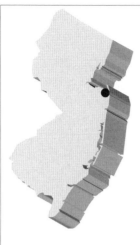

Mount Mitchill Scenic Overlook
Atlantic Highlands, Monmouth County
Phone: (732) 842-4000

Hours: Open daily 8 A.M. to dusk
Fees: None
Facilities: Portable restrooms, playground; memorial to Monmouth County residents who died in the September 11, 2001, terrorist attacks on the World Trade Center

Directions:
From the North: Take the Garden State Parkway to Exit 117 and follow Route 36 east to the Navesink Avenue/Scenic Drive jughandle. Take the jughandle and proceed to the park entrance.

From the West: Take the New Jersey Turnpike to Exit 10 and follow signs to the Garden State Parkway. Take the Parkway south to Exit 117 and follow directions above.

From the Southeast: Take Route 36 north and follow directions above.

TRAIL

Although there are no formal trails, a small walkway loops around the overlook.

TRIVIA

Mount Mitchill is the highest point on the Atlantic seaboard between southern Maine and the Yucatan Peninsula in Mexico.

Viewing area at the Mount Mitchill Scenic Overlook

6

Twin Lights State Historic Site
First for Fresnels

OVERVIEW

Any trip to the Sandy Hook Unit of the Gateway National Recreation Area [see #7] should encompass an excursion to the Twin Lights State Historic Site and the Navesink Twin Lights. For those not predisposed to vertigo, a trek up the narrow, winding staircase to the top of the north tower affords a fantastic view of Sandy Hook, Raritan Bay, and the Manhattan skyline. But be careful on the stairs: A steel bulkhead likes to reach down and clunk the heads of inattentive climbers.

HISTORY

Perched on a 200-foot-tall cliff in the Atlantic Highlands, the lighthouse, once known as the Navesink Lightstation, was for many years the primary lighthouse of New York Harbor.

A lot of firsts took place here. The original towers, built in 1828, were the first in the country to be equipped with the latest invention, the Fresnel lens, brought from France in 1841 by U.S. Navy Commodore Matthew Perry.

A new set of towers, built in 1862, was later the first to use kerosene lamps and the first to be powered by electricity. It was also here that Italian inventor Guglielmo Marconi first demonstrated his wireless telegraph in 1899.

Twin Lights State Historic Site
Lighthouse Road
Highlands, NJ 07732
Monmouth County
Phone: (732) 872-1814
Web site: www.twin-lights.org

Hours: 10 A.M. to 5 P.M. Memorial Day through Labor Day; 10 A.M. to 5 P.M. Wednesday through Sunday, September through May
Fees: None
Facilities: Museum, interpretive exhibits, gift shop, and restrooms

Note: Before you go, be warned that the steep road leading to the lighthouse is off-limits to oversized vehicles and trailers.

Directions:
From the North: Take the Garden State Parkway to Exit 117 and follow Route 36 east for approximately 11 miles into the Atlantic Highlands. Once there, follow signs to the lighthouse. You've gone too far if you've crossed the bridge.

From the West: Take New Jersey Turnpike to Exit 10 and follow signs to the Garden State Parkway. Take the Parkway south to Exit 117 and follow the directions above.

From the Southeast: Take Route 36 north, cross the bridge, and follow signs to the lighthouse.

According to the Twin Lights Historical Society, the Pledge of Allegiance was first recited here on April 23, 1898. The U.S. Army also experimented with the Mystery Ray (radar) at the Twin Lights in the 1930s.

The U.S. Coast Guard decommissioned the towers in 1949. In 1954 Atlantic Highlands Borough took over administration of the lighthouse and, with the Twin Light Historical Society, established a park and museum. The Twin Lights became a New Jersey State Historic Site in 1962.

MUSEUM

The building in which the museum is housed was built in 1862. It served as the light keeper's quarters and storage rooms, and linked the two towers. Today it contains exhibits on the Life-Saving Service, navigation techniques, a history of lighthouses, and lighthouse keeping.

A brief walk up the cast iron, spiral staircase leads you to the top of the north tower, where you are treated to a fantastic panorama of the area clear to Manhattan Island. It gets pretty windy here, even on a good day, so hold on to your hat.

Following are some of the outdoor exhibits at the museum.

MARCONI'S TRANSMISSION

An audio exhibit to the left of the North Tower marks the spot where Marconi conducted his wireless transmission on September 30, 1899.

According to the recording made by Marconi's daughter, Gioia Marconi Braga, the transmission was originally to have carried news of the 1899 America's Cup races. But the races were delayed. Instead, Marconi's radio report carried news of a naval review celebrating Commodore George Dewey's victory at the Battle of Manila Bay in the Spanish-American War.

According to Braga, Marconi's invention was met with skepticism by the lighthouse keepers and signal servicemen. "They listened silently, spat meditatively, and looked at him as if he had lost his mind," she said.

◄ *A Navesink Twin Light*

THE "MYSTERY" CANNON

At the front of the lighthouse is a very old, very rusty cannon. According to the exhibit, this is the "Twin Lights Mystery Cannon," unearthed when the lighthouse was being built. To this day, no one knows the cannon's owner or origin. The name etched on the cannon, "J Lopez," once briefly thought to be that of a Spanish pirate, turned out to be the name of the man who was lighthouse keeper when the cannon was discovered.

Twin Lights Mystery Cannon

FRESNEL LENS EXHIBIT

On exhibit in the lighthouse's power station is a Fresnel lens that was installed in the South Tower in 1898. The light produced by the new 9-foot, electric arc lamp was the equivalent of 25 million candles, and could be seen 22 miles away by day and up to 70 miles away at night.

Invented by Frenchman Augustine Fresnel, the key feature of the Fresnel lens wasn't the oil, kerosene, or, later, electricity, used for illumination, but the glass surrounding the lamp: It was cut in sets of prisms, providing a powerful illumination.

Fresnel lenses came in seven sizes, or "orders." The largest, a first-order lamp, was used for primary landfall areas, and was at least 7 feet high and 72.5 inches in diameter. The smallest, a sixth-order lamp, was 18 inches high and 11.75 inches in diameter. These were used in bays and shoals, or on wharves and piers.

Two Fresnel lamps were installed at the Twin Lights lighthouse. The light in the North Tower was a second-order revolving light; a first-order fixed light was installed in the South Tower. Why the difference? According to lighthouse historians, the first-order lens warned ships that they were nearing land. The second-order light gave notice to ships that they were approaching a bay and headland along the coast.

THE LIFE-SAVING SERVICE STATION

Near the North Tower is a small boat shed with brown cedar shakes and a whitewashed double door. This was the Spermaceti Cove Station of the country's Life-Saving Service, one of the first built when the service was initiated in 1848. The stations were positioned up and down the Atlantic coast, from Sandy Hook to Cape May.

The precursor of today's U.S. Coast Guard, the Life-Saving Service was established to aid survivors whose vessels were either wrecked by the dangerous shoals and shallow narrows leading into New York Harbor, or ran aground on sandbars or beaches. New Jersey's coast is extremely dangerous: Between 1839 and 1848, the government estimated that 158 vessels were wrecked offshore.

Rescuing shipwreck survivors—in any century—is risky business. In the 19th century rescuers either rowed a surf boat to the ship or, if the seas were too rough, used a "breeches buoy"—a canvas bag designed like a very large pair of Bermuda shorts. The buoy was sent over to the wreck via a line shot from a mortar and fixed to the wreck. The person being rescued simply stepped into the buoy and was hauled back to shore.

The breeches buoy could only accommodate one person at a time. In 1848 Toms River resident Joseph Francis invented a metallic, enclosed, watertight "life-car" that could rescue up to five people at once. Like the buoy, the car was fixed to a line and pulled in.

Twin Lights from a distance

TRIVIA

According to local historians, residents complained the light emitted from the lighthouse's 9-foot electric arc lamp was so strong that their cows could not sleep, and failed to produce milk in the morning.

7

Sandy Hook Unit of the
Gateway National Recreation Area
From "Noble Bay" to Playland

OVERVIEW

To the native Lenni-Lenape, it was "Racko Rumwaham," meaning hunting grounds lush with fowl and fish. To English merchant Thomas Pownall, it was an Eden set in "a most noble bay," flanked by the gray waters of the Atlantic Ocean and Raritan Bay and the brooding cliffs of the Navesink Heights. To the Dutch settlers, it was "Sandy Hoeck," an appropriate name for the 6-mile barrier island jutting from the hunched shoulders of the New World.

By whatever name, the Sandy Hook Unit of the Gateway National Recreation Area, or "the Hook," has always attracted visitors. Besides swimming and sunning, hiking, jogging, and biking are major attractions. Windsurfers collect on blustery days year-round to challenge the gusts off Plum Island and Spermaceti Cove, and anglers bring their rods and reels to fish for bluefish, fluke, and striped bass off North and Chokeberry beaches.

Carved on its eastern, or ocean, side by winds and salt into dunes of pale beige sand dotted with sparse grasses, the island might appear barren to visitors. The Hook, which covers 1,665 acres, however, is a key nature center. Its western side, protected from the wild ocean winds, is rich with a variety of flora and fauna. Marshes and wetlands and thick forests are filled with red cedars, holly trees, and squat bushes filled with luscious purple nuggets called beach

Sandy Hook Unit of the Gateway National Recreation Area
1,665 acres
Sandy Hook, Monmouth County
Phone: (732) 872-5970

Hours: Trails and grounds are open year-round. Spermaceti Cove Visitor Center is open daily from 10 A.M. to 5 P.M. Lighthouse tours are offered by the New Jersey Lighthouse Society on weekends from mid-April to late-November. The Fort Hancock Museum is open 1 P.M. to 5 P.M. on weekends.

Fees: A $10 daily fee is required for beach-users from Memorial Day weekend through Labor Day. Beach visitors also have the option of buying a season pass for $50. All others coming to bird or visit the historic district can visit for free.

Facilities: Visitor center, interpretive exhibit, nature trails, and educational programs; seaside restaurant, concession stands open summer months only.

Directions:
From the Northeast: Take the Garden State Parkway south to Exit 117. Follow the exit ramp to Route 36 and proceed east for about 11 miles. Signs will point to the Gateway National Recreation Area.

From the West: Take the New Jersey Turnpike north to Exit 10 and follow signs for the Garden State Parkway. Take the Parkway south to Exit 117 and follow above directions.

From the Southeast: Follow Route 36 north. Once north of Sea Bright, follow signs to the Gateway National Recreation Area.

plums. Fat-breasted ducks—including scaup, American black ducks, and canvas-backs—seek haven here from the winter winds.

Because of its location in the migration corridor, this is an ideal place for birding. Thousands of birders flock here annually to enjoy the more than 300 species of birds found here. In the spring, the skies fill with passerines, from chunky, wide-winged raptors to tiny warblers whose stunning colors reduce seasoned birders to wide-eyed kids.

HISTORY

The Lenni-Lenape first used the island as their summer hunting camp. In turn, they were followed by Dutch and English settlers who originally found safe harbor on the south shores of Long Island, and came to appreciate its perilous channels as a natural gateway to commerce.

The island has also been history's accidental witness. During the Revolutionary War, the island's lighthouse was captured many times by both loyalists and patriots. Local legend also has it that Captain Kidd buried loot in the area.

Because of its proximity to New York's harbor, Sandy Hook was a key military point. The many forts built at its northern tip protected the entrance to New York Harbor through the 19th and 20th centuries. As technology changed and the need for improved ammunition grew, it became the U.S. Army's first proving ground. At the height of the Cold War, Nike missiles protected the Metropolitan area against any intercontinental ballistic missiles that might be launched from behind the Iron Curtain.

Today the missiles and soldiers are gone, and Sandy Hook harbors more pacific offerings. What was once a thriving military base is now a seaside getaway less than an hour's drive from Manhattan and approximately two hours from Philadelphia.

TRAILS, BEACHES, AND SIGHTS

"The Hook" is a mecca for nature hikers and birders. Where and how you start your tour is up to you. The park's hiking and biking trail brings visitors through some of the more popular nature areas, but you will still have to get off the paved road to really enjoy some of these.

One word of caution: The park's unofficial plant, poison ivy, is rampant. Take care not to brush up against it on narrow footpaths leading through the dunes.

PLUM ISLAND

Upon entering the park, find Parking Lot B, located seaside on your right. Park and cross the road to the swatch of narrow, sandy beach that is bayside. Plum Island, as this area is called—it probably got its name from the island's profusion of beach plums—is a favorite spot for windsurfers and the few sunbathers who prefer to eschew beachside for a quieter spot. If the tide is low enough, you'll find several species of shorebirds and seagulls combing the mud flats for treats, as well as the usual wetlands suspects of egrets and great blue herons. Willets and lesser and greater yellowlegs can also be found if the conditions are right.

Beach plum in bloom at North Beach in Sandy Hook

◀ *Sandy Hook Lighthouse*

SPERMACETI COVE

From Plum Island, drive north on Hartshorne Road to the Spermaceti Cove Visitor Center, located in what was the second Life-Saving Station overlooking the beach (the first is on display at the Twin Lights State Historic Site [see #6]). A boardwalk across the road takes you to a bayside deck, where you can watch for shorebirds, waders, and ospreys.

During the winter the cove provides shelter for brant and a profusion of wintering ducks, including hooded and common mergansers. The spring migration months can produce a few surprises here. In May 2002 there was spectacular fallout of American Redstarts.

To the right of the boardwalk is the park's holly forest. There is a trail here, but the forest, for conservation reasons, can only be accessed during one of the occasional tours led by a park ranger.

OLD DUNE TRAIL

This delightful trail is a 1-mile loop that starts and stops at the Spermaceti Cove Visitor Center. Along the way you'll ramble through part of an American holly forest to a freshwater marsh and the island's characteristic sand dunes. Watch for broom sedge, black cherry trees, Virginia creeper, greenbrier, and other plants that favor the island's dune environs.

The trail is also a good place to watch for spring and fall migrants, but take care: At one point, you must cross the island's hike/bike path. There is also a fair amount of poison ivy on the trail, so watch where you walk and what you brush up against.

HORSESHOE COVE

Horseshoe Cove, located farther north (park in Parking Lot L), provides more of the same avian offerings. Look for the osprey nest to the right of the boardwalk here. Unlike at Spermaceti Cove, you can wander off the boardwalk and stroll the beach.

Spermaceti Cove Visitor Center ➤

GUNNISON BEACH

I speak the naked truth: You might see more than you bargain for at Gunnison. Although the beach will offer up shorebirds like the rest of the beaches here, this one has, for years, been the preferred area for nude bathing. A sign at the entrance warns the weak of heart and modest that this is a "clothing optional" area.

At the entrance to the beach is Battery Gunnison. Built in 1904, the battery originally housed a disappearing six-inch caliber gun.

A museum in the battery's lower building outlines the history of ordnance at the fort. From time to time, a local World War II reenactment group demonstrates how the big guns were used.

NORTH BEACH

Sandy Hook's North Beach is the farthest beach on the island. Set beyond the proving ground, it's a good place to fish and to bird.

Follow the signs to Parking Lot K, which is where some trails begin. You can either stay straight and take Fisherman's Trail, which takes you to the beach and North Pond, or take one of two trails to your right.

The first trail brings you to the locust grove loop around the New Jersey Audubon observation platform. This is a spectacular place in spring. The beach plum explodes in white blossoms, and spring migrants, from raptors to warblers, abound.

Of course, if you don't feel like birding, just take the hikes to enjoy the scenery. On a good day you can get a clear view of the Verrazano Narrows Bridge that links Staten Island to Brooklyn, NY. You can also see clear to lower Manhattan.

If you take the North Beach trails, remember to heed the poison ivy.

From here, your journey takes you down Hartshorne Drive back toward the Fort Hancock Historic District.

Officer's Row at Fort Hancock Historic District ➤

FORT HANCOCK HISTORIC DISTRICT

A sign bearing the district's name, along with a monument in the form of a Nike missile, announces your arrival to the district. The monument, the central point of Guardian Park, was erected to honor six soldiers and four civilians killed in a non-nuclear Nike missile explosion in nearby Middletown on May 22, 1958.

Start your tour at the monument. To your left, along Hartshorne Drive, is "Officer's Row," where the fort's officers lived from 1898–1974. The buildings are all made of buff brick, a more expensive and durable construction material than red brick.

The house closest to you on the left, No. 20, was the hospital steward's quarters. Today it is home to the New Jersey Audubon Society's Sandy Hook Bird Observatory. The largest house in the compound, Building No. 12, was home to the fort's commanding officer (rank does indeed have its privileges). Building No. 1 houses a museum that is open from 1 P.M. to 5 P.M. on weekends.

There are more buildings across the parade ground. Building No. 27, to the left of the flagpole, served as bachelors' quarters; No. 26 was post headquarters; and No. 28 was the fort's jail—today, it houses the Fort Hancock Museum.

Other buildings of interest include the fort's Young Men's Christian Association (YMCA, No. 40), the Post Exchange (No. 70), the stable that housed army mules (No. 36), and fort firehouse (No. 51). During World War II, a side yard was used as a handball court. The "No Ball Playing" sign was added at a later time.

But today's Fort Hancock area is more than just a pretty place to visit. The U.S. Coast Guard's Sandy Hook Station is here, as is the James J. Howard Marine Sciences Laboratory. Part of the National Oceanographic and Atmospheric Administration (NOAA), the lab monitors commercial and recreational fishing activities. The Marine Academy of Science and Technology, located on Gunnison Road, is a high school.

SANDY HOOK LIGHTHOUSE

If this is your first visit to the Sandy Hook Lighthouse, you'll likely wonder: What's a lighthouse doing so far inland?

The truth is, when the lighthouse was built in 1764, the building sat at the shoreline. But time, tide, and the elements all contributed to its modern-day location.

Originally, the lighthouse was called the New York Lighthouse, since it had been built by New York merchants tired of their ships being wrecked by the dangerous shoals of Raritan Bay. Its strategic position made it very desirable to Continental and British forces during the Revolutionary War, and it was captured and recaptured by both sides.

The light has been extinguished only twice in its history. The first time was by patriot troops in 1776, the second during the coastal blackouts of World War II.

Declared a national historic site in 1964, the 103-foot-tall lighthouse, with its whitewashed tower and 7-foot-thick base, is said by lighthouse experts to be the oldest standing lighthouse in the country.

Dawn at Sandy Hook

BATTERIES AND PROVING GROUND

In the late 19th century the military sought to improve the speed in which large guns, primarily used to shell enemy ships off the coast, could be fired and reloaded. Machinery was designed that allowed the guns to be lowered for fast reloading. These "disappearing" guns were tested at the Fort Hancock proving ground. In service between 1874 and 1919, the proving ground was the Army's first.

Start your tour at Mortar Battery, across the street from the lighthouse on Hudson Road. Built in 1894, this battery housed 16 guns whose purpose was to destroy the decks of battleships.

Continuing down Hudson Road, you come to Battery Granger. Built in 1897, this was the fort's first counterweight disappearing gun battery.

Built in 1895, Battery Potter, your next stop, was the only steam-driven disappearing gun battery in the country.

To the left of Battery Potter is Nine-Gun Battery, which housed 9-, 10- and 12-caliber disappearing guns.

Nearby are the ruins of Battery Peck. These can be seen as you walk to the North Pond and New Jersey Audubon hawk watch platform.

Cannon at Fort Hancock

TRIVIA

British soldiers and local militia loyal to the Crown embarked for New York from Sandy Hook following their defeat at the Battle of Monmouth in June 1778.

8

Cheesequake State Park
Nothing to Do with Cheese

OVERVIEW

The 1,267-acre Cheesequake State Park is a mishmash of fresh- and salt-water marshes, cedar swamps, and pine and upland forests, making it ripe habitat for a wonderful assortment of birds and beasts, as well as more than 200 species of plants and shrubs.

There's a little of something for everyone in Cheesequake. Hook's Creek Lake is great for swimming in the summer and non-motor boating the rest of the year. Trails make for terrific hiking and biking year-round, and snowshoe trekking and cross-country skiing in the winter. There are shaded picnic centers for that outdoor cookout, playgrounds where the kids can enjoy a slide or jungle gym, and campsites for pitching the tent and roasting marshmallows after a hard day's fun.

If you're looking to bird, fall and spring are the best times to come to Cheesequake. Approximately 30 types of warblers, including the rare Cerulean Warbler, can be found in springtime. In the fall, watch for migrating raptors, including the rare peregrine falcon, rough-legged hawk, and bald eagle.

The park's interpretive center has an assortment of exhibits about the park's history and natural offerings, and free programs for school and youth groups.

Cheesequake State Park
1,267 acres
300 Gordon Road, Matawan, NJ 07747
(Mailing address)
Middlesex County
Phone: (732) 566-2161;
(732) 566-3208 – Interpretive center

Hours: 8 A.M. to 8 P.M. Memorial Day through Labor Day. 8 A.M. to dusk all other months. The interpretive center is open 8 A.M. to 4 P.M. daily from Memorial Day to Labor Day; 8 A.M. to 4 P.M. Wednesday to Sunday all other months.

Fees: $5 weekdays, $10 weekends from Memorial Day weekend through Labor Day weekend. Campsite fees: $15 per night, per site, with a six-person per-site maximum; $1 per person per night for group campsites. Group picnic fees are $50 per day, plus parking fees, between Memorial Day and Labor Day, and $75 per day all other months. There's a 50 percent cancellation fee.

Facilities: Visitor center, interpretive center, beach, several picnic centers, 53 campsites with modern sanitary facilities and hot showers, and playfields. Carry in/carry out program. Partially accessible to persons with disabilities: Call (732) 566-2161 for more information about access needs.

Directions:
From the North: Take the Garden State Parkway south to Exit 120. Turn right onto Laurence Parkway to Cliffwood Avenue and turn right. At the T-intersection, turn right onto Gordon Road; the park entrance will be on your right. *Alternate route:* If you're coming from the local area, take Route 34 south and make a left on Disbrow Road. Follow that road to the end and make another right. At the first light, make a left and follow the road into the park. Watch closely for the brown park signs, as a few stand beyond key turning points.

From the West: Take the New Jersey Turnpike north to Exit 10 and follow signs to the Garden State Parkway. Take the Parkway south to Exit 120 and follow the above directions.

From the South: Take Route 34 north and turn right at Disbrow Road. Follow the local directions above.

Wetlands at Cheesequake State Park

HISTORY

Cheesequake has been a state park since 1940. Because of its proximity to major highways in central New Jersey, it is among the easiest state parks to reach from the New York Metropolitan area.

Strange but true, the park was not named for the occasional mini-earthquakes that hit the area. Rather, "Cheesequake" is derived from the name of a Lenni-Lenape sub-tribe, the Chichequaas, or "upland" people. Over time, that name was drawn out to "Cheseh-oh-ke," and, eventually, to what it is today.

TRAILS AND SIGHTS

The park has five trails, all color-coded. Four—the Yellow, Red, Blue, and Green—are hiking trails, although joggers and some hard-core mountain bikers can be found tackling the steep slopes and staircases. A fifth trail, the White Trail, is a multipurpose trail frequented by cyclists.

Of the hiking trails, the Yellow Trail is the shortest and easiest. The Green Trail, on the other hand, is the longest and hardest. The Red and Blue Trails fall somewhere in between. The trails start from the parking area at the interpretive center, and take 20 to 90 minutes to hike. Detailed descriptions of the hiking trails follow.

Caution: As beautiful a place as it is, Cheesequake does carry certain dangers. Trails can be slippery, weather depending, so plan accordingly. There is a considerable amount of poison ivy, so become familiar with the shiny "leaves of three" before heading out.

Another danger is the poisonous Northern copperhead snake: It will bite if provoked. Any snake whose skin bears a chestnut-colored hourglass pattern is best avoided. When in upland areas and rocky hillsides, watch where you walk and where you place your hands.

You'll also want to wear sturdy boots, load up on insect repellent, snacks, and water, and consider carrying a walking stick, as some of the steeper inclines can be slick.

Interpretive center at Cheesequake State Park

YELLOW TRAIL

Just 1-mile long, the Yellow Trail is the park's shortest and easiest trail. A brochure, available at the interpretive center, points out trail highlights, including red oaks, sweet pepperbush, pitch pines, and sassafras.

The trail begins to the right of the parking lot at the center. You can either turn left and proceed clockwise, or go straight to a staircase that leads down to the 6-acre Hook's Creek Lake. At the lake, watch for osprey and waders like great egrets and great blue herons. You'll also see a good crop of arrow arum, a plant so named for leaves that resemble bright green arrowheads.

RED TRAIL

At 1.3-miles long, the Red Trail is moderately difficult. The trail loops up and down in a network of steep slopes and wooden staircases from the interpretive center through wetlands, upland forests, and pitch pine trees. Along the way, watch for bayberry, shadbush, and American holly.

At Gordon Field, the trail merges with the Green Trail. Said to be a former Lenni-Lenape site, the field today is home to a group campsite, comfort station, and picnic area.

BLUE TRAIL

At 1.9 miles, the Blue Trail is the second longest hiking trail in the park, and also one of the most challenging. Like the other trails, it winds up steep slopes and wooden staircases, then down to wetlands and boardwalks that serve as the border between the park's salt- and freshwater marshes.

This is a rugged but gorgeous trail. Look for Indian pipe (a native plant that appears clear in color because it lacks chlorophyll), cinnamon fern, salt-marsh grass, and a bayberry forest. There are also nesting boxes here for Eastern bluebirds.

The trail crosses Perrine Road to Perrine Pond, a former clay-mining site. To the left is an observation blind that overlooks the pond: Watch for herons and egrets in spring and summer; in fall and winter, watch for hooded and common mergansers.

From here the trail turns onto Museum Road, which leads back to the parking area and the interpretive center.

GREEN TRAIL

At 2.9 miles the Green Trail is the longest trail and the most challenging. Like the other trails, this route takes you up and down an assortment of slopes, wooden staircases, and boardwalks through each of the park's ecosystems.

One-half mile into the trail you'll come to a boardwalk, the center of which is dominated by a very large tree. This is the start of the park's hauntingly beautiful white cedar swamp containing trees that are at least 150 years old. While in the swamp, note the sphagnum moss that is prevalent in the area. The Lenni-Lenape used this absorbent natural material, commonly called peat moss, for diapers. During World War I, soldiers in the battlefield used it to dress wounds.

As you proceed, watch for the various swamp plants, including clammy azalea, bayberry, highbrush blueberry, curly-grass fern, Virginia chain fern, sweet pepperbush, and pitcher plant.

One mile into the trail you will come across sheep laurel, an evergreen that blooms reddish purple to deep pink in early summer. Sheep laurel is lovely to look at, but deadly to eat. In fact, its toxicity has earned it a less palatable name: lambkill.

After proceeding up—and down—through more forests and marshes, you'll enter an area filled with ferns and a dark, cooling canopy reminiscent of the Amazon River basin. The trail eventually leads you to a boardwalk with a wildlife viewing blind overlooking a marsh. Here is another good spot for viewing herons and egrets.

A small boardwalk continues over a stream of clay-colored mud and water dyed the color of tea, thanks to the cedars. This walkway has a tendency to wash out after spring rains, so take care. Eventually, the trail reverts back to a sandy path that leads to a service road and Gordon Field, where it connects with the Red Trail behind the interpretive center.

WHITE TRAIL

The 3-mile White Trail, a multipurpose trail for hikers and mountain bikers, is an alternative to the hiking trails. The trail starts at the park's visitor center, and loops around the Booth Field Group campsite. Take this trail in late spring and you'll be treated to blooming mountain laurel.

◄ *Cedar swamp at Cheesequake State Park*

ARROWSMITH POINT

If you're interested, park at the Spring Hill picnic site and walk to Arrowsmith Point. The site provides a good look at an osprey nest and a salt-water marsh that attracts numerous waders and shorebirds when the tide is out.

HOOK'S CREEK LAKE

If you enjoy angling, trout and catfish can be caught at Hook's Creek Lake. To the right of the lake is a gravel path, lined with pokeweed, which leads to a wildlife viewing blind where you can view a crabbing bridge and two osprey nests perched atop the marshes' salt hay and phragmites. The road beyond the crabbing bridge brings you to a triple-tiered Purple Martin house. You could also walk around to the far side of the lake and take the staircase to the Yellow Trail.

Again, be aware: The late-summer mosquitoes are so bad here that I've seen grown men run.

CAMPSITES

Too tired to trudge home and too cheap (or broke) to sleep in a motel? Try camping overnight.

From May 1 to October 31, the park offers weary travelers 53 tent and trailer sites complete with grills, picnic tables and fire rings, flush toilets, and showers. The Gordon Field campsite offers six sites that can accommodate up to 25 people each.

Remember, because this is a state park, alcoholic beverages are prohibited, and all trash must be packed out. Bring your own garbage bags.

TRIVIA

The park is the final destination of the American eel. Every February and March, the eels, hatched in the Sargasso Sea off Bermuda, make their way to the local waters while they are in the "glass eel" stage as 1-inch larvae. Scientists believe the larvae float on the sea currents to reach their ancestral home.

◀ *Sumac at Cheesequake State Park*

9

Allaire State Park
From Company Town to Living History Museum

OVERVIEW

Strange but true, the 3,000-acre Allaire State Park was once a self-contained company town. Today a number of the town's buildings have been preserved and transformed into an interpretive museum that gives visitors a glimpse into 19th-century life, complete with funeral and wedding reenactments.

But there's more to do at Allaire than enjoy a remembrance of things past. Visitors can camp and picnic, hike, bike, bird, horseback ride, ride a historic train, and paddle and fish in the waters of the Manasquan River.

HISTORY

Allaire State Park was initially an 18th-century forge called Monmouth Furnace. In 1822, New York industrialist James Allaire bought the furnace and renamed the property the Howell Works, after former operator Benjamin Howell. The furnace produced castings and pig iron that was subsequently shipped to Howell's New York foundry and used to build steamship engines and boilers.

For more than 30 years Allaire thrived as a company town with 500 residents. But the discovery of iron ore in Pennsylvania in 1848, combined with the

Allaire State Park
3,000 acres
P.O. Box 220, Farmingdale, NJ 07727
(Mailing Address)
Monmouth County
Phone: (732) 938-2371 – Park offices;
(732) 938-2003 – Interpretive center

Hours: State Park: 8 A.M. to 8 P.M. Memorial Day through Labor Day; 8 A.M. to 6 P.M. spring and fall; 8 A.M. to 4:30 P.M winter. Allaire Village: 11 A.M. to 5 P.M Wednesday through Sunday, Memorial Day to Labor Day; 10 A.M. to 4 P.M weekends spring and fall. Allaire Village Visitor Center: 10 A.M. to 5 P.M daily Memorial Day through Labor Day; 9:30 A.M. to 4 P.M Wednesday through Sunday the remainder of the year. Interpretive Center: 8 A.M. to 4 P.M daily, seven days a week, Memorial Day through Labor Day; 9 A.M. to 4 P.M remainder of the year.
Fees: $5 entrance fee weekends Memorial Day through Labor Day; $8 per cabin bunk a night; $15 per night per campsite; $25 per night per yurt
Facilities: Nature trails, interpretive center, visitor center, historic village, gift shops, camping, picnicking, birding, hiking, bicycling, Pine Creek Railroad

Directions:
From the Northeast: Take the Garden State Parkway south to Exit 98. Follow the brown signs to the park but take care! As soon as you toss in your fee at the local tollgate, keep to your left: The sign for Allaire State Park is *behind* the next exit sign. Turn right on County Route 524 and proceed 1.5 miles to the park's entrance.

From the West: Take the New Jersey Turnpike north to Exit 10 and follow the signs to the Garden State Parkway. Take the Parkway south to Exit 98 and follow above directions.

From the Southeast: Take Route 34 north to Route 524 and follow signs to the park entrance.

Village life at Allaire State Park

discovery of fuel coal, led to its eventual demise. In 1907 famous Hearst news-paper journalist Arthur Brisbane bought the property and rented out the village to various groups, including the Boy Scouts.

Brisbane died in 1936. Five years later, his estate deeded the village to the state. A nonprofit group was formed in 1957 to help the state establish the interpretive museum.

THE VILLAGE

An early-morning visit to Allaire Village is pure magic. The buildings are still shuttered, and the only sounds are the occasional birdsong and water rip-pling down the millstream. Eventually the tourists will come with their digital cameras and camcorders to shoot the costumed volunteers in their bonnets and waistcoats. Until then, it's just fun to stroll the grounds and pretend you're back in the 1830s.

Pond at Allaire State Park ➤

When you enter the village proper, you first come to a row of whitewashed brick row houses. Foundry workers and their families originally lived here. Today they comprise the village visitor's center. Inside are numerous exhibits explaining the village's history and the forging process.

As you leave the center, continue down the walk to a small, two-story brick building; this once was the foreman's house. Passing the sites of the former gristmill, polishing mill, and screw factory—all now no more than foundations—you arrive at the blacksmith shop. The next shop on your left is the bakery. The ovens are no longer used on a regular basis, but you can buy pastries baked by local businesses, tea, and coffee.

At the neighboring millpond, children 14 and under can try their luck at fishing. The house beyond the pond was once the home of the manager and his family. Behind the manager's house stands the enameling furnace, now a museum. What is left of the park's file mill stands across the path.

Return to the millpond and stroll up the path to the village green. The large brick building to your left was built in 1835 and accommodated a general store, drug store, and post office. Today it is a gift shop managed by the nonprofit Friends of Allaire Village.

Next to the general store is the carpenter's shop. It may seem peculiar for a forge village to have a carpenter's shop with a wooden kettle, but cast-iron products were made from patterns that were cut from wood.

As you leave the general store, look directly across the green. The large house you see was once home to the superintendent of works and his family. A dormitory wing was added in 1835 to house workers. Allaire lived here with his family after he retired in 1850.

Directly in front of the house are the foundations of the village charcoal depot and furnace office. As you face the house, look to your left. The small, white building was the carriage house and gardener's cottage. Today it houses various antique wagons and carriages.

Behind the carriage house is the horse and mule barn. Behind the barn stands the foundation of the slaughterhouse. The meat from livestock butchered here was sold in the general store. A reconstruction stands nearby.

On the far side of the green is the Episcopal church that served both as a parish and school. The belfry contains a bell that was cast at the town under

General store at Allaire State Park ▶

HOWELL WORKS
GENERAL STORE

NO BARE FEET
NO STROLLERS

Allaire's supervision. According to local legend, Allaire tossed three gold coins into the liquid ore to ensure the bell would always ring on pitch.

After visiting the church, you can either continue on to the Pine Creek Railroad or retrace your steps to the general store and turn left on the path. This will take you to the village furnace and the Yellow Trail.

TRAILS AND SIGHTS

Four color-coded trails—Yellow, Red, Green, and Orange—run through the park, all easy for leisurely walking or hiking.

YELLOW TRAIL

At one-half mile, the Yellow Trail is the shortest. Follow the signs to the village's lower level, and follow the path as it meanders alongside the Manasquan River through a serene floodplain forest. Along the way, look for indigenous plants, including skunk cabbage, cardinal flower, mountain laurel, jack-in-the-pulpit, black raspberry, trout lily, marsh marigold, and stinging nettle.

RED TRAIL

The 1.5-mile Red Trail, which can be taken near the nature center, loops through the described floodplain and upland forests rich with conifers.

GREEN TRAIL

The 4.5-mile Green Trail is an easy hiking/walking trail that will take you beyond the Route 195 overpass. It's also the back way to the village from the nature center parking lot. If you do take this, watch for various ducks and herons in the pond. Great blue and green herons are known to gather there, especially in late summer, when the pond is thick with duckweed.

ORANGE TRAIL

The 16.5-mile Orange Trail is a moderate multiuse trail that winds throughout the park.

◄ *Carpenter working in Allaire Village*

Pine Creek Railroad

While in the park take a ride on the Pine Creek Railroad, which is run by the New Jersey Transportation Museum. The railroad is the only small-gauge railroad operating in the state. The 14-minute ride loops twice around a track that is just three-quarters of a mile long. The oldest car, a caboose, was built in 1874. Some of the cars were used by the military at Pearl Harbor during World War II.

Campsites

Like other state parks, Allaire offers overnight accommodations, but with a difference. Besides the usual cabins and campsites for tents and trailers, there's a modernized version of the Mongolian yurt, a circular canvas tent set on wooden poles. With its wooden floor, skylights, and outdoor deck, campers can spend the night in modest comfort for $25.

TRIVIA

Strange but true, the death of James Allaire's first wife, Frances Duncan, is commemorated every March with a reenactment of her funeral.

Bike a barrier island ... "slip" into a marina ... learn Lenape ...

Part 2
Barnegat Bay Region

10

Cattus Island County Park
Boy Scouts and Privateers

OVERVIEW

Located in the central part of Ocean County, Cattus Island is a delightful, 300-acre haven of upland forest and tidal marshes. Actually located on a peninsula that separates Barnegat and Silver bays, the area isn't really an island; however, it temporarily becomes one when, at high tide, water fills its marshes.

Today the park features a 6-mile trail network for hiking and limited biking, and bayside areas for fishing, crabbing, and picnicking. There are also excellent opportunities for birding. More than 380 species can be seen throughout the year, including many pelagics, or seabirds, like shearwaters and storm-petrels.

The park is named for New York developer John V. Cattus, who built a retreat here in 1895.

HISTORY

According to local historians, Cattus Island was first settled by the Page family in 1763. Timothy Page was a privateer, albeit a young one—he was born in 1763—who helped lure British ships into Barnegat Bay through the old Cranberry Inlet during the Revolution. Its reputation as a retreat grew after

Cattus Island County Park
300 acres
1170 Cattus Island Boulevard,
Toms River, NJ 08753
Ocean County
Phone: (732) 270-6960

Hours: Trails are open daily from dawn until dusk. The Cooper Environmental Center is open daily from 10 A.M. to 4 P.M

Fees: None

Facilities: Interpretive center with classes for children and adults; nature trails and restrooms

Directions:

From the North: Take the Garden State Parkway to Exit 82 and proceed along Route 37 east toward Seaside Heights. Take the jughandle to County Spur 549 (Fischer Boulevard). Proceed about 3 miles to Cattus Island Boulevard. Turn right at the light, then turn left into the park.

From the West: Take Route 70 east to Route 571 and proceed to Spur 549. From there, follow directions above.

From the South: Take the Garden State Parkway to Exit 82 and follow directions above; or take Route 9 North to Route 37 and follow directions above.

Cattus purchased the island and turned it into a private haunt for fishing, hunting, and sailing.

Like many nature centers throughout New Jersey, Cattus Island is one of those success stories in which conservation won out over development. Ocean County officials purchased the tract in 1973, after state laws limiting wetlands development were initiated.

Opened in 1980, the 5,000-square-foot Cooper Environmental Center, named for local environmentalists A. Morton and Elizabeth Cooper, offers free walks and nature programs throughout the year.

Entrance to Cattus Island County Park

TRAILS

Five hiking trails are spread throughout the park. Most can be accessed from a mile-long, unpaved road. One warning about the trails: Several run through marshes overgrown with phragmites more than 6 feet tall that choke the paths and boardwalks; double-check trail conditions with the naturalists. The more adventurous among us will not hesitate to bushwhack.

If you prefer, you can walk straight down the unpaved road to the island's tip. The road passes through tidal marshes. Look for ospreys; great egrets; great blue, tri-colored, and green herons; black-bellied plovers; and clapper rails.

The road eventually ends at the "Scout Island," named for the bevy of Boy Scout projects performed here. Along the way you'll also see the foundation of the original house.

RED TRAIL (MARITIME FOREST LOOP)

The Red Trail starts on a boardwalk to your right as you approach the environmental center, and takes you past the parking and picnic areas through both upland forests and wetlands. En route you'll encounter typical upland vegetation, including gallberry holly, winterberry, red oaks, and pitch pine. While in the uplands, watch for various bird species, such as yellow warblers and ovenbirds, which are common sightings in spring and fall. Wood thrushes, catbirds, and mockingbirds are also common.

If you prefer to cut the walk short, take the 0.4-mile White Trail, or Swamp Crossing, where indicated, but recall the phragmites.

Also, a brief, wheelchair-accessible trail leads down the boardwalk and circles around the park's picnic center and playground.

THE ISLAND LOOP

The Island Loop, at 2.2 miles the longest trail in the park, feeds off the unpaved road beyond the wetlands and winds along the forest. The trail takes you to the tip of Mosquito Cove, where the estate's boathouse once stood. This was a popular place for winter ice-skating, and Cattus often slapped runners on his Barnegat Bay Sneakbox, a type of hunting skiff [see #11], to race across the ice. From here you proceed through forests of greenbrier and pitch pine and wetlands thick with those looming phragmites.

While in any Cattus Island wetlands, keep an eye out for swamp sparrows and saltmarsh sharp-tailed sparrows.

YELLOW TRAIL (CEDAR LINE SHORTCUT)

Follow the Yellow Trail through the forest if you want to trim your hike and return to the road, or just want *no mas* of the phragmites. This shortcut can also be accessed from the road.

ORANGE TRAIL (HIDDEN BEACH LOOP)

Located at the end of the road, the Orange Trail is a 0.7-mile trail that circles "Scout Island." The hike is mostly through wetlands and marshes.

TRIVIA

According to local historians, Cattus's retreat house, which burned down in 1973, held as many as 30 beds.

Wetlands in Cattus Island County Park ➤

11

Toms River Seaport Society Maritime Museum
Life-Saving and Sneakboxes

OVERVIEW

It's fitting that the Toms River Seaport Society Maritime Museum is housed on the estate of Joseph Francis. In 1843 Francis invented the "life-car," a covered boat used by the U.S. Life-Saving Service to rescue shipwreck survivors.

Today the Society, founded in 1976, is committed to its own form of life-saving: restoring and preserving old and historic wooden boats, many of which, like the Barnegat Bay Sneakbox and Jersey Skiff, were crafted to suit the community's maritime needs. On any day you visit you're sure to see one or two volunteers sanding a hull, varnishing a keel, or shooting the breeze in the museum yard.

A visit to the museum is a great way to cap your visit to the Barnegat Bay Area. Not only do you get a great history lesson about local maritime life, but Toms River itself is a thriving coastal destination, offering free community events throughout the year.

HISTORY

Toms River has a long relationship with the Barnegat Bay waters. The fishing community in Dover Township was founded in 1767. Local historians think the town was named for Tom Luker, an Englishman who ran a ferry service on

Toms River Seaport Society Maritime Museum
78 Water Street
Toms River, NJ 08753
Ocean County
Phone: (732) 349-9209
Web site: www.tomsriverseaport.com

Hours: 10 A.M. to 2 P.M. Tuesday and Saturday, except holidays; group tours arranged by appointment
Fees: Small donation requested
Facilities: Interpretive displays, gift shop, and parking area

Directions:
From the North: Take the Garden State Parkway to Exit 81 and follow Water Street to Hooper Avenue (or as one volunteer put it, "Come south on Hooper Avenue until your hat floats"). The museum will be on the corner on your left.

From the West: Take Route 70 east to Route 530 into Toms River to Water Street. Turn right and proceed to the museum and Hooper Avenue.

From the South: Take Route 9 into Toms River and turn right onto Water Street. From there, follow above directions.

what was known as Goose Creek. What happened to the apostrophe in Toms River, however, is a mystery.

The town saw its share of horrors during the Revolutionary War: In 1782 British troops raided the village and killed nine locals.

Toms River continues to be a thriving community, although the local fishing industry is now comprised of mostly charters for pleasure fishing and seaside tourism.

Sneakbox and life-car at Maritime Museum

THE MUSEUM

Located in the estate's small carriage house, the museum is filled with local nautical history. Of particular interest is the *Sheldrake*, a 12-foot camping sneakbox that was single-handedly sailed by F. Slade Dale from Bay Head, New Jersey, to Miami's Coconut Grove via the Intracoastal Waterway. It took Dale and Frank Coyle, Dale's sailing partner who commanded his own sneakbox, from October 1925 to January 1926 to accomplish the 1,500-mile journey. That was pretty good time, considering that Coyle had never before sailed a boat.

Other items on display include an adaptation of a Lyle gun, used to shoot the lifesaving lines to ferry life-cars or breeches buoys to rescue shipwrecked survivors, and several antique outboard engines.

SNEAKBOXES

For those who have never spent cold, fog-shrouded mornings peering out of a duck blind, the Barnegat Bay sneakbox is a Jersey original. Invented in 1836

Toms River Seaport Society Maritime Museum

for duck hunting (so you could "sneak up" on the fowl), the spoon-bottomed boat became a favorite among recreational sailors.

The original sneakboxes were no more than 12 feet long by 4 feet wide—barely the size of a touring kayak. Their round bottoms made them easy to pole in shallow water, yet stable enough for a hunter to pop up and fire a shotgun when necessary.

Today the sneakbox continues to be used by hunters and recreational sailors in a number of shapes and sizes and with improvements.

TRIVIA

The museum and gift shop are housed in what was once the living quarters of the estate's groom.

12

Island Beach State Park
"Don't Annoy the Osprey"

OVERVIEW

Rich with wide, white dunes and a variety of natural resources, Island Beach State Park is a haven of serenity compared to the bungalow-crammed beach towns you must pass through to reach it.

Although the park is crowded during the summer months, it's virtually deserted the rest of the year, offering an idyllic habitat for all sorts of recreation, including surf fishing, kayaking and canoeing, birding, biking, swimming and sun-worshipping, and even horseback riding.

The park deserves its self-touted reputation as the state's "natural treasure." Little maritime forests abound, harboring pitch pine, red cedar, American holly trees, and Atlantic white cedars. The dunes are rich with beach plum and bayberry bushes, and beach heather that, in late spring, blazes with golden blossoms.

The Sedge Islands, sitting in Barnegat Bay at the tip of the inlet, are a Marine Conservation Zone. The zone is an attempt to improve wildlife resources while providing human activities like fishing, waterfowl hunting, clamming, and paddling. Today the islands are home to nesting peregrine falcons, black skimmers, and the state's largest osprey nesting colonies.

Island Beach State Park
3,000 acres
P.O. Box 37, Seaside Park, NJ 08752
(Mailing Address)
Ocean County
Phone: (732) 793-0030 – Gate house, call 24 hours
a day; (732) 793-0506 – Park office

Hours: Park open daily from 7 A.M. to dusk Memorial Day through Labor Day; 8 A.M. to dusk all other times. Park office open 9 A.M. to 4:30 P.M.

Fees: Entrance fees are $6 weekdays and $10 weekends Memorial Day through Labor Day; $5 daily the rest of the year. Walk-ins and bicyclists can get in for free; an annual state park pass is $50. Sport fishermen must get a mobile sportfishing permit; call the park office at (732) 793-0506 for more information.

Facilities: Beach swimming, scuba diving, hiking, biking, kayaking and canoeing, sportfishing, and horseback riding. Picnicking allowed in Recreation and Southern Natural Areas only. Lifeguards are on duty 10 A.M. to 6 P.M. daily in summer season. No swimming is permitted once lifeguards leave their posts. Interpretive centers open through summer season only. The Northern Bathing Beach Pavilion hosts numerous nature tours and programs July through September. For more information, visit the following Web sites:

Jersey Coast Anglers Association: www.jcaa.org

New Jersey Beach Buggy Association: www.njbba.org

Save Barnegat Bay: www.savebarnegatbay.org

Friends of Island Beach: www.friendsofislandbeach.com

Directions:

From the North: Take the Garden State Parkway south to Exit 82. Proceed east on Route 37 through Toms River and cross the causeway to Island Beach. After the bridge, turn right onto Route 37 and proceed south through Seaside Park all the way to the park. The entrance will be directly ahead.

From the West: Take Route 70 east to Route 37 all the way onto Island Beach. Proceed through Seaside Park to the park entrance.

From the South: Take Route 9 north and turn right onto Route 37. From there, follow the above directions.

Osprey and nest at Island Beach State Park

HISTORY

Like Sandy Hook and the Atlantic Highlands, Island Beach was originally the hunting grounds for the Lenni-Lenape, and was later settled by European colonists. One property owner was William Alexander, commonly known as Lord Stirling, who purchased the property in the 18th century and named the land Stirling's Isle.

The island became known as a hunting and sport-fishing community by the mid-1800s. In 1846, in response to the increased number of ships using the bay—and wrecking on the treacherous shoals—three lifesaving stations were built.

In 1926 the island was bought by Henry Phipps, a partner in Andrew Carnegie's Pittsburgh Steel Company. He built three homes, with the intention of turning the island into a resort operated by the Phipps Barnegat Bay and Beach Company. That idea, however, died with the stock market crash of October 1929.

His dreams dashed, Phipps left the property in the hands of his foreman, Francis Freeman. Freeman was apparently as much an environmentalist as an entrepreneur. He continued to provide visitors with passes to the island, but under four conditions: "Leave things be. Don't trample the sand dunes. Don't pick the flowers. Don't annoy the osprey."

The state purchased the island from Freeman in 1953 for $2.7 million, and the park, as a state entity, opened in 1959.

TRAILS AND SIGHTS

Before you visit Island Beach State Park, remember: This gorgeous natural playground is 10 miles long. Concession stands and restroom facilities are open between Memorial Day and Labor Day, but you're on your own the rest of the year. The best thing is to bring a cooler packed with food and non-alcoholic refreshments. Don't forget drinking water. Dress appropriately, or carry clothing, like raingear, with you if skies look cloudy. Have suntan lotion handy.

Last but not least, do not—I say again, do not—forget the insect repellent. Be it May or October, Island Beach mosquitoes are as voracious as their counterparts in the Amazon Basin and Florida Everglades. Green-headed flies and ticks are also problematic.

Spizzle Creek

The park is separated into four areas: the Northern Natural Area, Recreation Area, Southern Natural Area, and Bayside Access Area. They are all described in the following pages.

A short note for bicyclists: Rejoice. Biking lanes run the length of the park.

Northern Natural Area

The Northern Natural Area is a 3.3-mile stretch that runs from the park's gate to Parking Area 13. As you pass the main gate, you'll come to what was once U.S. Life-Saving Service Station No. 14, one of the original stations built when the service was started in 1848. The building now houses the park's maintenance area. Visitors are not permitted, but you can read about it on the interpretive exhibit standing in the parking lot.

The Aeolium Nature Center is an interpretive center open between May and September. The short (0.2-mile) trail here introduces you to the park's barrier island ecosystem. You can also, if lucky, catch some interesting birds at the feeders; one Saturday morning, I spotted a pair of rose-breasted grosbeaks and a Northern towhee.

A 6-mile bridle path starts at the park visitor center (the Northern Bathing Beach Pavilion) and runs south to the island's end. The trail is open to equestrians from October through April. The park issues up to 20 equestrian permits at a time, and reservations must be made in advance.

If you have a horse but haven't checked out the trail here, do so. Nothing compares to a trail ride on the beach, especially when you know what you're doing.

Recreation Area

Leaving the Northern Natural Area, proceed south to the first of two bathing areas. If it's a swim you're after, park, grab your towels and cooler, and take advantage of the white, sandy beaches here.

If you're out to roam, park at the Fisherman's Walkway trail near Parking Area 7. A wheelchair-accessible boardwalk provides a brief and enjoyable walk to the beach and an observation deck. This is a good place to watch for

Observation blind ➤

shorebirds in the spring and fall. A nearby access road lets permitted surf-fishermen access the beach in their four-wheel drive vehicles.

Want a respite from all that sun and surf? Cross the road, and walk the short Tidal Pond Trail, which takes you through a pastiche of phragmites and hardwoods to an enclosed bird observation blind overlooking Barnegat Bay. You've got a good chance to spot glossy ibises and great blue herons, chattering kingfishers, ospreys, and maybe—if you're lucky—myrtle and cerulean warblers.

SOUTHERN NATURAL AREA

The Southern Natural Area runs for 3 miles, from Parking Area No. 13 all the way down to Barnegat Inlet. There are no lifeguards, so the area is off-limits to swimming. But you can surf fish and walk the dunes.

The 0.1-mile boardwalk trail takes you through freshwater wetlands to a fantastic view of white dunes covered with beach grass, beach heather (which blooms a fantastic gold in late May), and seaside goldenrod. Along the way,

Prickly pear

take note of a freshwater wetland area: Cranberries grow there. You'll also want to be on the alert for interesting bird species, like brown thrashers.

Farther along the road is the Forked River Interpretive Center. Open May through September the center provides exhibits on the island's ecosystems, along with a collection of sneakboxes. The center is in the former U.S. Life-Saving Station No. 112.

The Emily deCamp Herbarium, your next stop, houses more than 400 plants found on the island. Janet's Garden offers a look at various local plants, including inkberry and prickly pear cactus, which produces a delightful fuchsia-colored flower in early fall.

Two short trails, one to the ocean and one to Johnny Allen's Cove bayside, (see Bay Access Area section following), provide a shady and sandy walk through sheltered dunes rich with shadbush, sassafras, beach plum, bayberry, holly, and pitch pine. Watch for myrtle and black-throated blue warblers.

Drive to the last parking area, Parking Area 23, if you want to visit the very end of the island, 1.5 miles from here. If you don't have a vehicle permit for the beach, you'll have to walk. It's worth the effort, since it provides you with a great view of the Barnegat Lighthouse.

The southern tip of the island is also where you want to go to see harlequin, long-tailed ducks, buffleheads, and king eiders in the winter time.

BAY ACCESS AREA

This area actually runs the length of the entire park, so you may want to visit its various stops while you're exploring the other areas. For simplicity's sake, we will again start at the park's main gate.

As soon as you pass the park's entrance you'll come to a parking area for Reed's Road on your right (the lot is directly across the street from the park's maintenance area). The 0.4-mile-long route is a sandy path (no vehicles allowed!) that takes you to the bay.

The next nature stop, located at the park's 3.6-mile mark, is the Tidal Pond and bird observation blind discussed earlier.

Tice's Shoal, across the road from Fisherman's Walkway at the 4.9-mile mark, is another brief (0.1 mile) trail that leads to the bay.

The trail at the Forked River Interpretive Center splits, leading to either the ocean or Johnny Allen's Cove.

Farther south, stop at either Parking Area 19 or 20 and take the Spizzle Creek trail. A right turn on the trail takes you to the creek's observation blind: Watch ospreys, black-crowned night herons, little blue herons, and glossy ibises.

If you turn left, the trail takes you bayside to the remnants of an old boat shed and a spectacular view of the Barnegat Lighthouse.

View of Barnegat Lighthouse from Spizzle Creek trail

THE SEDGE ISLANDS

Bringing your paddling gear? The bayside kayak launch is opposite Parking Area 21. From here, you can paddle out to the Sedge Islands for an up-close and personal look at the flora and fauna there.

The Sedge Islands Marine Conservation Zone starts as a thin strip bayside of Parking Area 13, then balloons around the islands to the Barnegat Inlet.

Paddlers can take one of two water trails. The Marsh Elder Trail circles the Marsh Elder Island. It's a challenging route because sand bars at low tide may

◄ *Johnny Allen's Cove trail*

force you to get out and portage. The easier Little Boy Trail to the south brings you through deeper waters around Sea Dog Island.

The standard paddling time for both trails is two to three hours. As always, whenever paddling the ocean, mind the tides, know where you're going, try not to paddle alone, and—yes, I know this is "mother" speaking—do not partake of alcohol.

TRIVIA

Ahoy! Like "The Hook" [see #7], Island Beach played a role in the Revolutionary War. American privateers would snatch British supply ships, then either sail them to Toms River, or up the Barnegat Inlet to Tuckerton.

13

Double Trouble State Park
Double Pinelands Pleasure

OVERVIEW

The 7,881-acre Double Trouble State Park is pure fun for anyone who wants to experience the state's Pinelands National Reserve, a massive, 1-million-acre portion of southern New Jersey encompassing seven counties. Once the site of a cranberry and lumber business, the property was purchased by the state in 1964.

The park's highlights include picturesque peat and cranberry bogs; Cedar Creek, a 9-mile creek that flows into Barnegat Bay; and a 19th-century village that has been restored and turned into a living history museum. Tours of the sawmill and cranberry packinghouse are available, and cranberry farming continues to this day.

If you can, try to visit the park during fall cranberry harvest season. There are few more spectacular scenes than a field of blazing cranberries set against the brilliance of a hardwood forest whose leaves are turning.

HISTORY

Double Trouble was the site of a sawmill and lumber company from the mid-1700s to the early 19th century, when the first cranberry bog was built. In

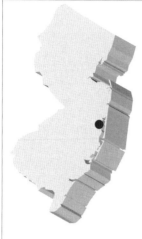

Double Trouble State Park
5,000 acres
P.O. Box 175, Bayville, NJ 08721 (Mailing Address)
Ocean County
Phone: (732) 341-6662

Hours: The park grounds are open daily from dawn to dusk.
Fees: None
Facilities: Hiking, biking, birding, picnicking, historic village, and paddling

Directions:
From the North: Take the Garden State Parkway south to Exit 77. Turn left onto Route 619 and follow signs to the park.

From the Southeast: Take the Garden State Parkway north to Exit 77, turn left onto Route 619, and follow signs to the park.

From the Southwest: Follow Route 70 east to Route 614. Proceed southeast to Route 530, and travel east to Route 618. Follow signs to the park.

1904 Edward Crabbe purchased the property. Phasing out the lumber business between 1910 and 1925 in favor of increased cranberry production, Crabbe planted some 225 acres of cranberry bogs.

The state bought the property from the Crabbe family in 1964. Many of the buildings were restored in the mid-1990s.

TRAILS

Double Trouble State Park has a 1.5-mile network of unmarked nature trails that thread the park's forests of pitch pine and white cedar like tunnels in

Cedar Creek at Double Trouble State Park

a rabbit warren. The paths are excellent for cross-country skiing in winter. In early spring watch for the tiny Northern azure butterfly.

The park's village stands just beyond the park's entrance. Preserved buildings include the old schoolhouse, cranberry packinghouse, company store, bank and cook houses, sawmill, three pickers' cottages, and the foreman's residence.

TRIVIA

How Double Trouble got its name is unclear. Local historians have two theories. Some say the name stems from the 18th century, after heavy spring rains twice washed away the Cedar Creek dam. Others insist that workmen repairing the dam found not one leak, but two.

14

Forked River State Marina
Barnegat Bay Gateway

OVERVIEW

This 125-slip marina, poised along the Forked River Estuary, is an ideal place to enjoy the fishing and boating pleasures of Barnegat Bay, the Intracoastal Waterway, and the Atlantic Ocean. Its Route 9 location makes it an easy destination for weekend sailors traveling from the New York Metropolitan area.

You can enjoy the marina even if you don't have a boat. It's a great place to take photographs, especially on a bright day, when the reflections of the crafts shimmering in the water offer some creative shots.

While visiting the marina, watch for various seagulls and terns hovering over the water, or sitting on the marina stanchions like ornaments.

A visit to the marina can be combined with visits to Tuckerton Seaport [see #18] and Great Bay Boulevard Wildlife Management Area [see #19].

HISTORY

Forked River was New Jersey's first state-operated marina. It was built in the 1930s—at the height of the Great Depression—to help improve Ocean County's troubled economy.

Forked River State Marina
311 South Main Street
Forked River, NJ 08731
Ocean County
Phone: (609) 693-5045

Hours: Office is open 8 A.M. to 4 P.M. Monday through Friday, year-round.

Fees: None if you're just walking around.

Facilities: 125 slips for vessels 20- to 55-feet long; picnic area, restrooms; water, electricity, cable television, and phone hookups; bait and tackle shop, restaurant, repair facilities, and gas and diesel fuel are nearby.

Directions:
From the North: Take the Garden State Parkway south to Exit 74 and Route 614 (Lacey Road). From Route 614, turn south onto Route 9. Follow the highway about 9 miles south of the Toms River area. The marina will be on your left—you can't miss it.

From the West: Take Route 70 east to Route 614 and proceed east to Forked River. Turn left onto Route 9 and proceed north; the marina will be on your right.

From the South: Follow Route 9 north through Forked River. The Marina will be to your right on the north side of the town.

TRIVIA

The marina's administration building, built in 1990, sits on the site of a former full-service gas station.

Reflection in water at Forked River State Marina

15

Eno's Pond County Park
From Ice House to Wonderland

OVERVIEW

Eno's Pond County Park in Lacey Township is one of those gems travel experts often overlook as a destination. The 28-acre county park is a wonderful place to stop and visit, whether simply to stretch your legs en route to the Jersey Shore, or to spend an entire day. One reason for its appeal is its tranquil, easy-to-walk nature trail; its large, family-friendly picnic and playground area is another.

HISTORY

Eno's Pond has been part of the Ocean County Park System since 1998. The original pond was the result of a wood and earthwork wagon crossing, built long ago to accommodate traffic crossing Bridge Creek. In the 1880s local hotelier Byron Eno enlarged it to serve as a source of ice for his nearby Riverside Hotel and Casino. Remember, this was the time prior to iceboxes and refrigerators!

TRAILS

Two nature loops—a 1-mile walking trail indicated by red markers, and a shorter, wheelchair-accessible trail designated by blue markers—thread

Eno's Pond County Park
Lacey Township
Ocean County
Phone: (609) 971-3085
Web site: www.co.ocean.nj.us/parks

Hours: Open daily 7:30 A.M. to one-half hour prior sunset daily
Fees: None
Facilities: Nature trails, some of which are wheel-chair accessible; playing fields, picnic area with grills, playground, and restrooms

Directions:
From the North: Take the Garden State Parkway south to Exit 74 and bear right onto Route 614 (Lacey Road). Cross Route 9 and pass the Captain's Inn. The park entrance is on the left, near the end of the road.

From the West: Take Route 70 east to Route 614 and follow the directions above.

From the South: Take Route 9 north and turn left onto Route 613. Continue until you reach the park entrance.

through adjacent property owned by the Edwin B. Forsythe National Wildlife Refuge [see #20].

Both trails take visitors through typical Pine Barrens and uplands habitat. Along the way you'll encounter red cedars, beach plums, persimmons, bayberry, and pitch pine, not to mention the pond. Two observation decks on either side of the pond give you a great look at the local wildlife, including numerous waders and ducks.

Eno's Pond

RED TRAIL

The Red Trail starts to the right of the park entrance, in the Forsythe section, and runs along a narrow dirt path through upland forest. Along the way, watch for bayberry, pitch pine, and what is called a "wolf tree"—a tree with limbs greatly spread out. You'll also see greenbrier and American holly trees, along with the foundation of a house razed by fire in the 1950s.

An observation blind provides an excellent view of the creek: Watch for ospreys and waders in the spring, and a variety of ducks in the winter months.

A boardwalk at Eno's Pond gives visitors the chance to observe various birds, including Great Blue Herons and egrets.

Trees of interest on the trail include southern red oaks, beach plums, and eastern red cedars. You'll also pass persimmon trees. This is as far north as this southern tree will grow.

Observation blind at Eno's Pond

Blue Trail

The Blue Trail is wheelchair accessible. It starts behind the ball field to the left of the park's entrance and loops around the park in a shorter, wider loop to Eno's Pond and two observation decks.

TRIVIA

Fire destroyed Eno's hotel in 1952, but the building that housed the casino still stands, and today is home to the Captain's Inn restaurant. You'll pass it on your way to the park.

16

Barnegat Lighthouse State Park
25 Cents an Acre

OVERVIEW

Barnegat Lighthouse State Park takes some time to reach, but it's certainly worth the trip. The park sits at the north tip of Long Beach Island (LBI), an appropriately named barrier island that has been a popular resort since the early 20th century. To reach the park, mainland visitors must take the causeway from Manahawkin into Ship Bottom, turn left, then keep driving ... and driving ... until the road narrows and they come to the end of the road. The 165-foot lighthouse stands there in its glory.

Today, visitors come year-round to picnic or walk the short, self-guided nature trail. It's a popular swimming beach during the summer months.

In winter, birders replace the two-legged sun-worshippers. Bundled up to protect themselves from the bay's driving winds, they huddle on the fisherman's jetty to get a good glimpse of long-tailed ducks, harlequin, king eider, and Northern gannets.

An amusing aside: During World War II, my parents almost bought land on LBI. But my father was heading to the Pacific, and the future seemed uncertain. At 25 cents an acre, that land would have been a steal.

Barnegat Lighthouse State Park
P.O. Box 167
Barnegat Light, NJ 08006 (Mailing Address)
Ocean County
Phone: (609) 494-2016

Hours: Park grounds are open daily from dawn to dusk. Lighthouse hours are 9 A.M. to 4:30 P.M. daily during summer months, Wednesday to Sunday, spring and fall, and 9 A.M. to 3:30 P.M. on weekends November to April. From July to September, the lighthouse is open until 9:30 P.M. on Saturday, and every second Wednesday.

Fees: None for the park, but adults and children 12 and older must pay a $1 fee to visit the lighthouse between May and September.

Facilities: Picnic area, nature trail, swimming, and fishing.

Directions:

From all points: Take Route 72 east across the Manahawkin causeway into Ship Bottom. Turn left onto Route 607, and proceed north approximately 6 miles.

THE LIGHTHOUSE

The 165-foot, first-order lighthouse you see today is not the original. The first, built in 1835, was a 40-foot tower containing a fifth-order light. When shore erosion toppled it into the sea in 1856, Congress authorized the U.S. Army Corps of Engineers to build a larger, first-order lighthouse. The light remained in operation until 1944, closed for repairs in 1988, and reopened to the public in 1991.

Barnegat Lighthouse ➤

Anyone who dares to hike up the 217-step winding staircase will be rewarded with a spectacular view of the ocean, bay, and estuary, not to mention Island Beach State Park [see #12], which is just across the channel.

TRIVIA

The Barnegat Lighthouse, like those in Absecon and Cape May, was built by Army Lieutenant George C. Meade, who, in the Civil War, went on to command the Army of the Potomac at Gettsyburg in 1863.

17

U.S. Coast Guard Station, Barnegat Light
"You Don't Have to Come Back"

OVERVIEW

Like their brothers and sisters up and down the coastline, the crew members of the U.S. Coast Guard Station at Barnegat Light are there to help boaters who get in trouble while navigating the challenging waters around the inlet.

Tours are not available on a regular basis, and a tall, chain-link fence surrounds the property, but there is an interpretive exhibit outlining the Coast Guard's role in protecting the American coast over time.

HISTORY

The U.S. Coast Guard was established in 1915 and is the descendant of the original U.S. Life-Saving Service formed in 1848.

The service was started to assist the many shipwrecks that occurred during the early maritime years up and down the treacherous Jersey coast. Between 1839 and 1848, government officials estimated that 158 vessels were wrecked offshore on the dangerous shoals and sandbars leading into New York Harbor.

Coast Guard stations were established along the state's Atlantic coast, from Sandy Hook to Cape May. Over the years some of the stations have been moved and improved, but the Guard's presence has been a comforting constant.

U.S. Coast Guard Station, Barnegat Light
6th Street and Bayview
Barnegat Light, NJ 08007
Ocean County
Phone: (609) 494-2680

Hours: Open daily from dawn to dusk
Fees: None
Facilities: Interpretive exhibit; tours available by appointment

Directions:
From all points: Take Route 72 east across the Manahawkin causeway into Ship Bottom. Turn left onto Route 607, and proceed north to 6th Street. Turn left. The station is at the corner of 6th Street and Bayview Avenue.

Although lifesaving techniques have, over time, advanced from the days of Joseph Francis's life-car, saving lives is still one of the most dangerous occupations on earth. Still, despite often life-threatening conditions, Coast Guardsmen selflessly honor the Service's unofficial motto: "You have to go out, but you don't have to come back."

The present station at Barnegat Light replaced an earlier building that was located on 7th Street, near the ocean.

TRIVIA

A little tombstone at the station marks the grave of Sinbad, a well-known mixed-breed pooch adopted by a Coast Guard cutter crew in 1938. Sinbad's subsequent international travels and World War II adventures made him the subject of a *Life* magazine story. He served 11 years at sea before being retired to Barnegat in 1949, where it was said he enjoyed his liquor at Kubel's Bar. Sinbad died in 1951, and was buried beneath the station's flagstaff.

Vessel at the U.S. Coast Guard Station at Barnegat Light

18

Tuckerton Seaport
Baymen and Decoys

OVERVIEW

Tuckerton Seaport is probably the most comprehensive and ambitious attempt by the state of New Jersey to illustrate its rich bayshore heritage, from Lenni-Lenape times to today.

Visitors can spend hours prowling the seaport's buildings and nature trail, or attending one of its many interpretive programs held throughout the year.

In the fall the seaport hosts an annual decoy and gunning show that offers more than 500 exhibits and vendors, along with skeetshooting, duck calling, decoy carving, and retrieving contests.

Combine your visit to the Tuckerton Seaport with a tour of nearby Great Bay Boulevard Wildlife Management Area [see #19].

HISTORY

The Tuckerton area was originally settled by Europeans in the 17th century. Because of its proximity to Little Egg Harbor and Barnegat Bay, it was the haunt of colonial privateers during the Revolutionary War as well as a bustling 18th-century port. In 1791 President George Washington designated it a U.S. port of entry.

Tuckerton Seaport
120 W. Main Street
P.O. Box 52
Tuckerton, NJ 08087
Ocean County
Phone: (609) 296-8868
Web site: www.tuckertonseaport.org

Hours: 10 A.M. to 5 P.M. daily April through October; 11 A.M. to 4 P.M. weekends November and December (call to confirm hours of operation); closed January through March

Fees: $8 adults and children 13 and over, $6 seniors 62 and older, $3 children 6 to 12 years old, free for children 5 and under. Parking and docking are free with paid admission; tour packages are available for groups of 15 and more.

Facilities: Museum, gift shop, restaurant, and restrooms; 27 floating docks

Directions:
From the North: Take the Garden State Parkway south to Exit 58 and follow Route 539 southeast to Tuckerton to Route 9. Turn south and proceed to Tip Seaman Park.

From the West: Take Route 70 east to Route 72 east to Route 539. Proceed on Route 539 and turn right at Route 9. The Seaport is about one-half mile on the left. You've gone too far if you pass Tip Seaman Park.

From the South: Take the Garden State Parkway north to Exit 50 to Route 9 north. The seaport will be on your right once you cross into Tuckerton Borough.

By the end of the 19th century, the primary industries here were boat making, fishing, oystering, and clamming. Although today's commercial emphasis is on tourism, there remains a strong sense of the community's maritime heritage.

THE VILLAGE

Tuckerton seaport is a work in progress. Seventeen buildings had been opened when I visited, with 16 more planned.

Your tour starts at the Tuckerton Yacht Club, home to the seaport's admission office, gift shop, and an interactive exhibit about the Jacques Cousteau National Estuarine Research Reserve project, which encompasses 115,000 acres in the Mullica River–Great Bay area. The project is funded by the National Oceanic and Atmospheric Administration (NOAA), and is a collaboration between the seaport, the reserve, and Rutgers University.

When you leave the Yacht Club, turn right and proceed down the gravel path beyond the 1930s Skinner-Donnelly houseboat, to Joe Dayton's Sawmill

Tuckerton Seaport

and the Perrine Boat Works, where visitors can watch master boatmakers—many of them the sons of master boatmakers—build sneakboxes using traditional tools. More than 3,600 of the classic boats were created at Perrine's.

From the Boat Works return to the Yacht Club. Follow the boardwalk around the dock and wetlands to Parson's Clam and Oyster House, where an interpretive display shows how the shellfish were harvested through the mid-20th century.

Your next stop, the Bath House, holds the seaport's restrooms. These are closed off-season; use the facilities in the Yacht Club.

As you move on, you come to Napoleon Kelly's Oyster House, which contains exhibits and a display on the history of oystering.

Your next two stops are replicas of the decoy-carving shops of late master carvers Hurley Conklin and Jay C. Parker. These are the actual workshops of some of the area's best decoy carvers; their works can be purchased. Barnegat decoys, by the way, are made of white cedar, hollowed out so as not to weigh down a sneakbox, and carved with flat bottoms so they bob better in the bay.

Decoy carver at work

Now follow the boardwalk around Pharo's Landing to the Hester Sedge Gun Club. The building is a replica of a waterfowler's hunting shack circa 1940, complete with period icebox and stove. The decor, from the decoys in the mudroom to the two-bunk bedrooms, reeks of manliness. The table is set for dinner and post-hunting "medicinal" refreshment.

When you leave the club, turn left and continue around the boardwalk. The *Melody II* is an authentic, 38-foot charter fishing boat built in 1957; today it takes parties on tours of Tuckerton Creek. Look into the shallow creek water; if you're lucky, you'll see one or two diamondback terrapins basking just below the waterline.

Behind the *Melody II* sits Tucker's Island Lighthouse. Built in 1868, the original third-order lighthouse collapsed into the bay at the height of a 1927 storm. This replica contains various exhibits about local history.

Want to learn the language of the Lenni-Lenape? Here's your chance. An interactive exhibit teaches you simple words and phrases, like "Ktalenixsihac," ("Do you speak Lenape?"), "Taltane," ("I don't know"), and "Weli Kishku," ("It's a good day").

You can also learn a little Lenape folklore. According to the Lenape, the world was formed on the back of a turtle. Its upper shell formed land, from which sprang a tree. One of the tree's roots was man; the other, woman. In fact the Lenape called the first Europeans "salt men" because they came from the sea.

A small stairway brings you to the light tower, where you can venture outside and enjoy a panoramic view of Tucker's Creek and the surrounding land.

When you leave the lighthouse, turn left and proceed to the seaport's Crest Fishery building, where an exhibit depicts the history of the area's pound fishing industry.

To the left of the fishery is the Hotel deCrab, which presents an exhibit about the local resort industry. Built in 1847, the original Hotel Crab (the name was changed for the sake of exoticism) once served as a refuge for shipwreck survivors in the Long Beach Island community of Harvey Cedars. The hotel went out of business after the U.S. Life-Saving Service was initiated, so the hotel's owner, Capt. John Tilton "Tilt" Fox, relocated it to Beach Haven, all the way on the other side of the island. Fox eventually sold the hotel for $650 in 1917. It was torn down in 1984.

Tucker's Island Lighthouse ➤

The next building, the Marshelder Gun Club, is a replica of the original club-house on Marshelder Island in Little Egg Harbor Bay. Formed in 1955 the club was referred to as the "Cadillac of gun clubs." Inside are exhibits on other local gun clubs, not to mention an impressive display of 19th- and 20th-century shotguns and decoys.

From here, return to the Yacht Club and exit the front entrance. The hunting shanty on your left is the former Barnegat Bay Decoy and Baymen's Museum, now an interpretive center. Decoy-carving classes are regularly held here. To the left of that building is Skeeters Seafood Café—a great place to grab a bite. The service is friendly and the fresh seafood is cooked to order.

Across the parking lot are two other structures. The Sunny Brae Salt Box is a historic building that houses the office of the seaport's education coordinator, while the Seacaptain's House is home to the seaport's administrative offices.

One interesting item worth checking out, although it's not part of the Heritage Trail, is the statue that stands on the corner of Route 9 and Great Bay Boulevard, behind the seaport sign. This is a memorial to the Improved Order of Redmen, Great Council of New Jersey. Erected during World War I, the statue originally stood in Camden and was relocated to Tuckerton in 1981. The Improved Order of Redmen is comprised of the descendants of American colonists who participated in the 1773 Boston Tea Party. Rather than stage political protests, however, Order members today raise money for charities.

TRIVIA

Tuckerton was called Clam Town until 1798, when Ebenezer Tucker hosted a banquet and persuaded the town fathers to change the name.

19

Great Bay Boulevard Wildlife Management Area
The Highway to Nowhere

OVERVIEW

Like those at Edwin B. Forsythe National Wildlife Refuge [see #20], the coves and marshes of the 3,965-acre Great Bay Boulevard Wildlife Management Area (WMA) provide excellent birding opportunities. This is especially true during the spring migration months, when the tidal marshes offer all sorts of winged finds, from black-bellied plovers, red knots, and ruddy turnstones, to dowitchers and willets.

It's also a great place for fishing. Popular catches include striped bass, weakfish, fluke, flounder, sea bass, and bluefish.

HISTORY

The area was first inhabited more than 2,000 years ago by an indigenous tribe that predated the Lenni-Lenape. It was first settled by Europeans in the 17th century.

During the Revolutionary War, Colonial privateers ventured from the inlets to capture British ships, then sailed them up either Tuckerton Creek or the Mullica River in the Pine Barrens, where supplies were removed and distributed to Colonial militia.

Great Bay Boulevard Wildlife Management Area
3,965 acres
Tuckerton, Ocean County
Phone: (609) 259-2132 – NJ Division of
Fish and Wildlife

Hours: Open daily from dawn to dusk
Fees: None
Facilities: Birding, fishing, clamming, and hunting;
boat ramps available at private marinas nearby

Directions:
From the North: Take the Garden State Parkway south to Exit 58 and follow Route 539 to Tuckerton. From there take Route 9 south to Great Bay Boulevard.

From the West: Take Route 72 southeast to Route 539. Continue on Route 539 south through Tuckerton to Route 9. At Route 9, proceed south and turn left onto Great Bay Boulevard.

From the South: Follow Route 9 north into Tuckerton. Turn right onto Great Bay Boulevard.

In the 1840s a fish factory was established on what is now called Fish Island. Thanks to contamination, however, the fish factory shut down some 140 years later.

In 1928 the state had an ambitious plan to build a highway that would cross the marshes from Tuckerton to Great Bay, to Brigantine, all the way to Atlantic City. However, an unpalatable mix of poor soil conditions, political sparring, and the start of World War II forced an end to construction, and the 7-mile highway, which came to be called the Tuckerton Cutoff, was never built beyond Great Bay.

Tidal marshes at the Great Bay Boulevard Wildlife Management Area

In 1976 the state bought 4,670 acres from the J. Howard Smith Fish Company and inaugurated the wildlife management area.

TRAILS

The Great Bay Boulevard WMA area can be easily driven, hiked, biked, or paddled. Leaving Tuckerton Seaport, turn left on Route 9, then make another left onto Great Bay Boulevard. The management area itself begins beyond a residential development on your right.

Soon after this development you'll come to the area's first bridge. Park in the parking lot, hike to the bridge's apex, and look down to the area from which you walked. You'll see a clump of trees on your left: This is the sight of a 2,000-year-old shell mound, the remnants of that earlier, unknown tribe. (By the way, the later Lenni-Lenape used the purple part of the clamshell for their money, known as "wampum.")

Continue down the boulevard. Little Egg Harbor will be on your left, Great Bay on your right. At low tide during the spring and summer months, watch for

Osprey platform at the Great Bay Boulevard WMA

shorebirds like lesser and greater yellowlegs, sanderlings, plovers, and waders. Near the 6-mile marker on your right, you'll find an osprey platform; you may see a nesting pair in late April or early May.

Slightly to the left of the platform, and closer to the road, are the remains of a houseboat that was once owned and inhabited by noted local bayman Ray Kennedy. Kennedy bought the boat from a local clammer for $150 in 1945 and lived there until 1962.

As you continue down the boulevard, you'll pass several marinas, where, for a fee, you can put in a kayak, canoe, or sneakbox. You'll also cross two one-lane bridges. The stoplights that control bridge traffic seem to take forever to change.

Toward the end of the boulevard, in the distance on your right, you'll find two imposing structures. The first is the remains of a fish factory once locally known as "the Stink House." Built in the 1930s, the factory processed menhaden, an oily fish used to make, among other things, fertilizer and cosmetics additives.

The second structure was once a U.S. Life-Saving Station, built in the 1930s after the Tucker's Island station, along with its lighthouse, was washed away in 1927. Today, the large, white compound is a field station, along with its lighthouse, for Rutgers University's Institute of Marine and Coastal Sciences.

When you reach the end of the road, park and walk around the barrier to the beach. Here you'll find another good place to observe shorebirds and pelagics.

Field station for Rutgers University's Institute of Marine and Coastal Sciences

TRIVIA

Tuckerton gained national fame when, during World War II, German Nazis tried to erect an antenna on nearby Mystic Island. The plot was foiled when the military confiscated the antenna.

Paddle a tidal marsh ... love a lighthouse ... bird, bird, bird! ...

Part 3
Absecon and Cape May Regions

20

Edwin B. Forsythe
National Wildlife Refuge
Migrant Motel

OVERVIEW

Whether stopping en route to Atlantic City or Cape May, or making it your final destination, the trails along the impoundments and coves of the Edwin B. Forsythe National Wildlife Refuge—it's called "Brigantine" or "Brig" for short, after its Brigantine Headquarters Division—make for a great outing.

Set on estuaries that separate it from Atlantic City, the refuge's 46,000 acres—a combination of coastal wetlands, uplands, and shore habitats—serve as an avian hotel for thousands of birds that migrate along the Atlantic flyway every spring and autumn.

Its ponds and surrounding bays and coves are also a winter home to thousands of snow geese that migrate from Canada and the Arctic Circle. That's not all: According to the Nature Conservancy, the refuge is winter home to 30 percent of all brant and American black ducks migrating along the eastern flyway. The refuge falls under the auspices of the U.S. Fish and Wildlife Service. Approximately 4,000 acres in the Barnegat Division are managed by the Nature Conservancy.

Just a word before you go: The refuge is sometimes closed for either management activities, such as controlled burning, or for hunting in the fall and winter. Call ahead or check the Web site to be sure it's open.

Edwin B. Forsythe National Wildlife Refuge
46,000 acres
Box 72, Great Creek Road
Oceanville, NJ 08231 (Mailing Address)
Ocean and Atlantic counties
Phone: (609) 652-1667
E-mail: forsythe@fws.gov
Web site: http://forsythe.fws.gov.

Hours: Trails are open daily from dawn to dusk, but can be closed on certain days for hunting in the fall, and for periodic controlled burns and other management tasks. Call before you go, or check the Web site. Headquarters are open weekdays from 8 A.M. to 4 P.M.

Fees: $4 per car admission fee, although a current Federal Waterfowl Stamp will give you free access.

Facilities: Brigantine Division offers nature trails, a picnic area, a boat ramp, observation towers, self-service visitor information and restrooms (Note: There are no restrooms on Wildlife Drive), paddling, fishing, crabbing, hiking, office, and auditorium. Barnegat Division offers nature trails, paddling, fishing, crabbing, and birding.

Directions (Brigantine Headquarters Division):

From the North: Take the Garden State Parkway south to Exit 48 and turn onto Route 9 south. Turn left onto Great Creek Road (third traffic light) and proceed into the refuge.

From the West: Take Route 30 east to Pomona and turn left onto Route 575 (Pomona Road). Turn right at the next traffic light onto Jimmie Leeds Road, and follow directions above.

From the South: This is a little tricky. Driving north on the Garden State Parkway, take the service area exit for the Atlantic City Service Area. From here, take the service road to Jimmie Leeds Road. Follow Jimmie Leeds Road to the fork in the road and turn left onto Great Creek Road. Follow this into the refuge.

Wildlife Drive in Forsythe's Brigantine Headquarters Division

HISTORY

Forsythe's Brigantine Headquarters Division, near Oceanville, was established in 1939. The Barnegat Division, consisting of several smaller wildlife areas between Brick Township and Manahawkin, and at Holgate at the southern tip of Long Beach Island, was established in 1967. They were separate and distinct refuges before they were combined and given the Forsythe name in 1984.

TRAILS

BRIGANTINE HEADQUARTERS DIVISION

Wildlife Drive

The one-way, 8-mile Wildlife Drive can be driven, biked, or hiked. Before you start your tour, go to the information kiosk and take a copy of the Wildlife Drive tour guide. Points of interest presented in the guide are marked by numbered wooden ducks along the drive.

The route takes you primarily around several impoundments bordering ponds and estuaries, where you can find shorebirds and waders, including green herons and glossy ibises. A peregrine falcon nesting site is set out in the middle of one pond and, if you're lucky, you'll also see a bald eagle or two.

Before you turn down Wildlife Drive, continue straight to Gull Pond, where an observation tower overlooks the pond, neighboring Doughty Creek, and the South Pool. The tower provides a good view of migrant ducks from November through January, including American black ducks, green-winged teal, and hooded mergansers.

Proceeding down Wildlife Drive, you'll cross the South Dike, which separates a freshwater pool and a brackish pool. When the tide's down, watch for shorebirds, including dunlin, sanderlings, greater and lesser yellowlegs, glossy ibises, egrets, and herons.

As you continue you'll pass the West Pool, a good gathering place for migrating waders and shorebirds in the fall; in winter look for American black ducks and brant.

Turtle Cove is next. Again, this is a salt marsh that attracts numerous brant and American black ducks in the winter. In spring look for spawning horseshoe crabs, which attract hundreds of shorebirds that feed off their eggs.

Your next stop of interest will be the south tower. The wind can gust fiercely at its top, but you'll get a great view of the surrounding marshes.

You then come to the East Pool, a 700-acre pool that is immensely popular with sandpipers and plovers from August through September.

The North Pool is a popular spot for snow geese November through January. Congregating on the waters, they look like white puffballs.

As you approach the end of the drive, the trail turns into an upland forest, where you can usually get a good glimpse of migrating songbirds. At the end of the drive you can either turn right, toward Route 9, or turn left and return to the start of the refuge to take advantage of the nature trails.

Nature Trails

Brigantine's four short nature trails give visitors a taste of the refuge's habitats.

Akers Woodland Trail is located at the refuge's parking area. It's a quarter-mile self-guided loop that takes visitors through woodlands, named for local

Snow geese in the Edwin B. Forsythe National Wildlife Refuge

naturalist James F. Akers. This is an excellent place to look for warblers during the spring and fall migrations.

Backdropped by a spectacular view of the Atlantic City skyline, the half-mile Leeds Eco-Trail loops through marshes and forested uplands: Watch for egrets, a variety of hawks, and fiddler crabs. Most of the trail is a wheelchair-accessible boardwalk. The trail begins at the start of Wildlife Drive.

Jen's Trail is a 0.75-mile loop located toward the end of Wildlife Drive, beyond the North Pool. The loop takes you through upland woods similar to those seen on the Akers Woodland Trail.

Songbird Trail can be taken either from Jen's Trail as a 2.5-mile hike, or from behind refuge headquarters for a longer, 4-mile trek. Again, this is a walk through uplands where warblers can be rampant in the migration months.

BARNEGAT DIVISION

The Barnegat Division starts approximately 40 miles north of Oceanville at the deCamp Wildlife Trail in Brick. The most extreme end of the division is a 4-mile stretch of dunes at the very bottom of Long Beach Island in Holgate.

For the sake of convenience, the Barnegat Division points of interest are detailed starting with the most northern trail in Brick, and continuing south to Holgate. Directions will also be given for each point of interest.

deCamp Wildlife Trail

This mile-long woodland trail is located at the intersection of Mantoloking and Adamston roads in Brick.

Directions:

From the North: Take the Garden State Parkway south to Exit 88 and Route 70 east. Make a right at Cedar Bridge Avenue (Route 528). Cedar Bridge Avenue turns into Mantoloking Road. The trail is at the intersection of Mantoloking and Adamston roads.

From the West: Take Route 70 east and follow the directions above.

From the South: Take Route 9 north to Toms River and proceed north on Route 549 to Route 528 and follow directions above.

Eno's Pond

The 1-mile nature loop at Eno's Pond [see #15] is a partnership between Ocean County Parks and Recreation and the refuge; one-half of the trail is on refuge property adjacent to the county park. The trail winds through pinelands and includes an observation blind where visitors can watch waders, ducks, and other species.

◄ *Akers Woodland Trail in Brigantine*

Directions:

From the North: Take the Garden State Parkway south to Exit 74 and bear right onto Route 614 (Lacey Road). Cross Route 9 and pass the Captain's Inn. The park entrance is on the left, near the end of the road.

From the West: Take Route 70 east to Route 614 and follow directions above.

From the South: Take Route 9 north until you reach Route 614. Turn left and continue until you reach the park entrance.

Barnegat Observation Platform

The Barnegat Observation Platform lets visitors get a good look at the various birds that enjoy flocking, feeding, and nesting in freshwater wetlands.

Directions:

From the North: Take the Garden State Parkway south to Exit 63. Take Route 72 east to Route 9. Make a left on Route 9 and proceed north to Bay Shore Drive. Turn left onto Bay Shore Drive. The platform is between Ridgeway and Edison avenues.

From the West: Take Route 72 east and follow directions above.

From the South: Take Route 9 north and follow directions above.

Bridge to Nowhere Fishing Area

Anglers will enjoy this nature area.

Directions:

From the North: Take the Garden State Parkway south to Exit 63 and take Route 72 east to Route 9. Proceed on Route 9 north to Stafford Avenue and turn right. Continue to the end of the road.

From the West: Take Route 72 east and follow directions above.

From the South: Take Route 9 north and follow directions above.

Cedar Run Fishing Area

Cedar Run is another good fishing area.

Directions:

From the North: Take the Garden State Parkway south to Exit 63 and Route 72 east to Route 9. This time, turn right and proceed south on Route 9 to Cedar Run and Dock Road. The fishing area will be on your left.

From the West: Take Route 72 east and follow directions above.

From the South: Take Route 9 north and follow directions above.

Parker Run Fishing Area

Parker Run is another good area for anglers and birders. When finished here you can move on to the nearby Graveling Point Fishing and Observation Area.

Directions:

From the North: Take the Garden State Parkway south to Exit 58 and take Route 539 east to Route 9 north, away from Tuckerton. Follow Route 9 to Dock Road in Parkertown and turn right.

From the West: Take Route 72 east to Route 539 and proceed south to Route 9. Follow directions above.

From the South: Take Route 9 north to Dock Road in Parkertown and turn right.

Graveling Point Fishing and Observation Area

You can combine this trip with a visit to the Tuckerton Seaport [see #18] and the Great Bay Boulevard Wildlife Management Area [see #19] or the Parker Run Fishing Area (above).

Directions:

From the North: Take the Garden State Parkway south to Exit 58 and turn left onto Route 539. Continue to Route 9 and turn right onto the highway. Proceed south on Route 9 to Radio Road in Tuckerton and turn left. The area is at the end of the road.

From the West: Take Route 72 east to Route 539 and proceed south to Route 9. Follow directions above.

From the South: Take Route 9 north to Radio Road in Tuckerton and turn right. The area is at the end of the road.

Holgate Unit

This little strip of barrier island is a prime nesting spot for piping plovers, so visiting is discouraged from April 1 through August 31. However, visitors are invited to enjoy the local flora and fauna at all other times of the year. Birding, hiking, and fishing are the prime recreations. To get here, take the Manahawkin causeway onto Long Beach Island, turn right, and just keep going until you reach the end of the island.

Holgate Unit of the Edwin B. Forsythe National Wildlife Refuge

TRIVIA

The refuge is named for the late Edwin B. Forsythe, a U.S. Congressman who was also a conservationist.

21

U.S. Coast Guard Station, Atlantic City
Continuing the Tradition

OVERVIEW

Perched on the windy intersection of Clam Creek and Absecon Inlet, under the shadow of the Trump Marina Hotel and Casino and Sen. Frank S. Farley State Marina [see #22], the 40-plus men and women of the U.S. Coast Guard Station, Atlantic City, perform search and rescue missions, enforce maritime law, and monitor marine environmental protection over a 250-square-mile area.

There are interpretive displays outside the compound, and the leisurely walk from the casino and marina to the station offers a view of the Atlantic City skyline. For security reasons, visitors cannot access the actual station grounds unless calling ahead for an appointment, but the small museum in the station lobby is worth a look.

HISTORY

The area's first Life-Saving Station was built in 1849 and was located downtown at the corner of Connecticut and Pacific avenues. In 1878, following a congressional act to improve the coast's lifesaving operations, it was moved to Absecon Lighthouse, where a larger station was built in 1884. It

U.S. Coast Guard Station, Atlantic City
Intersection of Routes 30 and 87
(Brigantine Boulevard)
Atlantic City, NJ 08410
Atlantic County
Phone: (609) 344-6594

Hours: Open daily from 8 A.M. to 5 P.M. but call ahead; a sign advises you not to enter unless you are "authorized personnel."
Fee: None
Facilities: Interpretive exhibit outside; museum depicting station's history inside

Directions:
From all points: Take the Atlantic City Expressway into Atlantic City. Take the purple "Marina" exit straight to the Trump Marina Hotel and Casino, at the intersection of Routes 30 and 87 (Brigantine Boulevard).

returned to Pacific Avenue at the turn of the 20th century. The present station was built here, at Brigantine Boulevard, in 1938.

It may also be noted that, prior to 1878, the station was manned entirely by volunteers.

TRIVIA

According to the state, the station, along with its sister station in Ocean City, annually handles about 400 search-and-rescue calls.

U.S. Coast Guard Station, Atlantic City

22

Sen. Frank S. Farley
State Marina
Boating Among the Bandits

OVERVIEW

The Sen. Frank S. Farley State Marina is the nautical gambler's dream: The marina, located on Clam Creek, is adjacent to the Trump Marina Hotel and Casino. Boaters can simply slip their ships into a berth and step into Atlantic City's world of one-armed bandits and poker tables. Landlubbers can sit and enjoy the fresh air and view of the Atlantic City skyline.

HISTORY

Built by the state in the late 1950s to revitalize the city's pleasure-boating industry, the marina nearly sank as a result of budget cuts 30 years later. But officials took a gamble and entered into an agreement with billionaire investor Donald Trump and Trump Castle Associates that put the marina under the care of Trump's hotel and casino operations.

The end result was a win-win for the state, pleasure boaters, and the House of Trump. The old marina was demolished and replaced with a spiffy 640-slip marina that can accommodate vessels of up to 300 feet.

Sen. Frank S. Farley State Marina
Trump Marina Hotel and Casino
600 Huron Avenue
Atlantic City, NJ 08401
Atlantic County
Phone: (609) 441-8482

Hours: The marina office is open 7 A.M. to 10 P.M. May 15 to June 30, and 7 A.M. to 12 A.M. from July 1 to Labor Day. Hours vary throughout the rest of the year.
Fees: If you plan to boat in, call ahead for slip fees.
Facilities: 640 boat slips with connections for water, cable, phone, and electric service; restrooms, private showers, laundry facilities, and office. Hotel and casino are just steps away, if you want to chance the turn of a hopefully friendly card.

Directions:
From all points: Take the Atlantic City Expressway to Atlantic City and follow the purple "Marina" signs to Trump Marina Hotel and Casino.

SIGHTS

The slips—and restrooms, for that matter—are off-limits to the public, but visitors can stroll the marina walkway. Afterward, you can try your luck at the casino's gaming tables, or continue your walk to the nearby U.S. Coast Guard Station [see #21].

TRIVIA

The marina is named for the late Frank S. Farley, an Atlantic City Republican who served in the state assembly and senate.

Sen. Frank S. Farley State Marina

23

Tuckahoe Wildlife Management Area
"Dark Waters, Shy Deer"

OVERVIEW

Straddling Atlantic and Cape May counties along the Tuckahoe River, the 14,393-acre Tuckahoe Wildlife Management Area (WMA) is a fun place to visit, whether you're birding, boating, hunting, or fishing. The area also provides shotgun and bow hunters with ranges to hone their skills, and there's a training area for hunting dogs.

Paddling or boat fishing? Put in at the ramp in Tuckahoe. The Tuckahoe River leads to Great Egg Harbor Bay. The fishing itself here is juicy: Catches include largemouth bass, pickerel, yellow perch, sunfish, eel, white perch, striped bass, fluke, and flounder.

HISTORY

Land purchases by the state in 1933 and 1940 resulted in Tuckahoe. The money used for the purchases came from money gained from the sale of hunting and fishing licenses and waterfowl stamps.

Tuckahoe is also known as the Lester G. MacNamara WMA. MacNamara was a director of the state's Division of Fish and Wildlife in the 1950s and 1960s.

Tuckahoe (Lester G. MacNamara)
Wildlife Management Area
14,393 acres
Atlantic and Cape May counties
Phone: (609) 628-2103 – NJ Division of
Fish and Wildlife

Hours: Open daily from dawn to dusk
Fees: None
Facilities: Office with brochures and information about the area; shotgun and archery ranges, dog-training area, boating ramp

Directions (main office and trails):
From the North: Take the Garden State Parkway south to Exit 20 to Route 50 north and proceed to Tuckahoe Road (Route 631); a tavern will be on your right. You'll see a brown and white state sign for the park on your left. Take that road into the park. The park office is in a small compound beyond the shotgun shooting range.

From the South: Take Route 9 north to Route 50, and follow the directions above.

From the West: Take Route 49 east through Tuckahoe to Route 50 south. Turn left onto Route 631 by the tavern and follow signs.

Directions (to Griscom Mill Road Extension from the main office):
Return to Route 631, turn right onto Route 50, and proceed north through Tuckahoe. You'll cross a small bridge into Corbin City, a small rural town complete with wandering chickens and the occasional cat napping along the roadside. Griscom Mill Road will be on your right; watch for a small white schoolhouse. Take Griscom Mill Road through a small residential area to the dirt road; this is the start of the driving trail.

Reservoir in the Tuckahoe Wildlife Management Area

TRAILS

There are two one-way driving loops you can drive, bike, or walk. One is a 3-mile loop drive near the WMA office off Route 50 in Tuckahoe. The second is a 5-mile loop off Griscom Mill Road in nearby Corbin City.

Both loops provide scenic overviews of marshes (which make up 72 percent of the area), meadows, lakes, and ponds. Watch for waders, like great blue herons and great egrets, American bitterns, rails, and kingfishers. During the spring and fall migration seasons you can find literally thousands of shorebirds, including dowitchers, red knots, curlews, ruddy turnstones, and willets.

While driving, beware of the frogs that tend to vault across the road when you least expect them.

TRIVIA

According to state historians, "Tuckahoe" was the Lenni-Lenape name for the area, meaning "where dark waters run deep and deer are shy."

Trail entrance in the Tuckahoe WMA

24

Corson's Inlet State Park
Sublime Relaxation

OVERVIEW

The only thing Corson's Inlet State Park offers is a relaxing time. Unlike Atlantic City, there are no casinos or flashy entertainers. Unlike nearby Wildwood, there are no amusement parks.

What you will find, however, area 350 acres of peaceful coastline, where the dunes are ripe for strolling or sunbathing, waters are fresh for fishing and crabbing, and flat terrain—the trademark of New Jersey's Outer Coastal Plain—is perfect for biking and jogging.

Birders will find piping plovers, black skimmers, and least terns here, so don't forget the binoculars and spotting scope. During migration months watch for monarch butterflies and dolphins.

HISTORY

The park was established in 1969 in an effort to save the area from the clutches of developers.

TRAILS

There are two trails, each about 1-mile long, which run through the park's 98-acre Strathmere Natural Area. Both take you on a leisurely stroll through the

Corson's Inlet State Park
350 acres
Strathmere, Atlantic County
Phone: (609) 861-2404 – Belleplain State Forest, from which the park is managed

Hours: Open daily from dawn to dusk
Fees: Boating fees of $5 daily, $50 annually
Facilities: No office, just a great bridge for fishing and crabbing, dunes for walking, a beach where you can either sit and sunbathe or swim, and a boating ramp

Directions:

From the North: Take the Garden State Parkway south to Exit 25, and follow Roosevelt Boulevard (Route 623) east to West Avenue in Ocean City. Turn right onto West Avenue and proceed to 55th Street. Turn right onto Ocean Highway (Route 619) and follow the road to Rush Chattin Bridge. Don't cross the bridge! Turn left into the parking lot immediately before the bridge.

From the South: Either take the Garden State Parkway to Exit 25 and follow the directions above, or take the "slow poke" route: Route 621 north to Route 619 north of North Wildwood.

phragmite-laced dunes to the beach. Along both, you'll be treated to the usual sights found in the Jersey dunes: cordgrass, bayberry, poison ivy, and seaside goldenrod.

TRIVIA

From Corson's Inlet State Park, you can eschew the highway for the leisurely and picturesque Ocean Drive south through the resort communities of Strathmere, Sea Isle City, Avalon, all the way to Stone Harbor and the Wildwoods to Cape May.

Beach at Corson's Inlet State Park

Along the way you can visit two other Coastal Heritage Trail sites: the Wetlands Institute in Stone Harbor [see #25] and the Hereford Inlet Lighthouse in North Wildwood [see #26].

There are two toll bridges along the route, so be sure you have a small amount of cash.

◄ *Trail in Corson's Inlet State Park*

25

The Wetlands Institute
Hands-On Nature Class

OVERVIEW

The 6,000-acre Wetlands Institute is the place to be for nature-lovers who want a bit of education along with their wanderings.

HISTORY

Founded in 1969 by Herbert Mills, the executive director of the World Wildlife Fund, the Institute sits smack dab in some of the most pristine wetlands this side of the Atlantic Ocean. The privately owned facility hosts numerous educational programs for children and adults.

The annual Wetlands festival, held in September, draws thousands to enjoy nature tours, exhibits, and entertainment.

TRAIL

Aquariums, butterfly gardens, and exhibits are all part of the institute's offerings, but probably the best feature is the trail that winds its way around the seaside tidal marshes. Visitors can take their own self-guided tour, using a

The Wetlands Institute
6,000 acres
1075 Stone Harbor Boulevard
Stone Harbor, NJ 08247
Cape May County
Phone: (609) 368-1211
Web site: www.wetlandsinstitute.org

Hours: 9:30 A.M. to 4:30 P.M. Monday, Friday, and Saturday; 9:30 A.M. to 8 P.M. Tuesday through Thursday; 10 A.M. to 4 P.M. Sunday, May 15 to October 15; 9:30 A.M. to 4:30 P.M. Tuesday through Saturday the rest of the year. Closed Christmas through New Year's Day.

Fees: Suggested donation $7 for ages 12 and up; $5 for ages 2 through 11
Facilities: Restrooms, gift shop, aquariums, nature and art exhibits, guided tours, and observation platform

Directions:
From the North: Take Exit 10B (at a traffic light) off the Garden State Parkway—the highway at this point is a local highway, complete with stop-lights—and turn left onto Route 657 east (Sunset Boulevard) toward Stone Harbor. The Institute will be on your right about 2.5 miles from the exit.

From the South: The fastest way to come from the Cape May area is to take the Garden State Parkway north to Exit 10B and make a right onto Route 657 east (Sunset Boulevard) toward Stone Harbor.

Wetlands Institute in spring

guidebook to follow markers along the way; join one of the regularly scheduled tours; or hire a naturalist for their own exclusive tour—call ahead for rates.

The trail starts to the left of the Institute, at the salt pond, and proceeds down a path lined with phragmites. Look for the osprey nest platform to your left: Ospreys typically nest May through July. The marshes are also a good place to look for herons, egrets, and the occasional glossy ibis that finds its way here to take advantage of shrimp and minnows at low tide.

The trail proceeds through a small upland area, where you can find red-winged blackbirds and tree swallows in the summer months, and yellow-rumped warblers in the fall. Trees and shrubs found here include bayberry, red cedar, and black cherry trees.

This is also a good spot to catch monarch butterflies during their fall migration. But be careful where you step in the spring: Diamondback terrapins lay their eggs on the higher ground, and their quarter-sized hatchlings often skitter along the trail.

◀ *Feathered friends dockside at the Wetlands Institute*

You have two choices at this point. If you continue straight on the path, you'll reach the pier overlooking Stone Harbor and Scotch Bonnet Creek; gulls and cormorants will often be seen. Alternatively, you can take the cutoff to your right and walk through the marsh. If you opt for this route, be sure to wear shoes with good traction: The silt is slippery after a good rain. Salt marsh cordgrass, pickle plant, and marsh elder ring the area, and you can spot tracks of some of the local animals, including raccoons and cottontail rabbits.

The path leads to a boardwalk, another good place to watch for waders like herons and glossy ibises. You can also try to scope out a clapper rail or two, but they are elusive birds; at best, you may only hear their trademark "clack-clack." The boardwalk returns you to the trail.

TRIVIA

The building that houses the Institute was designed to look like a 19th-century Life-Saving Station, complete with cedar shakes.

26

Hereford Inlet Lighthouse
True Victorian Charmer

OVERVIEW

With its straw-colored gingerbread frame and award-winning English-cottage gardens, it's hard to believe that the Hereford Inlet Lighthouse in North Wildwood almost bowed to the wrecking ball in the 1980s. Fortunately for us it was spared, thanks to the effort of a few local preservationists. Today the lighthouse receives more than 40,000 visitors annually, and is one of this seaside resort's most popular tourist attractions.

HISTORY

Styled in what is today called "Victorian-Swiss Carpenter-Gothic," the lighthouse was designed by Paul Pelz, designer of the Library of Congress and the Presidential Seal. When built in 1874 it was the only home on the island-town, which was then called "Anglesea," presumably after the Welsh fishing village. Lighthouse keeper Freeling Hewitt, a devout Baptist, held religious services in the modest parlor until the local church was built.

Hereford Inlet Lighthouse
111 North Central Avenue
North Wildwood, NJ 08260
Cape May County
Phone: (609) 522-4520
Web site: www.herefordlighthouse.org

Hours: 9 A.M. to 5 P.M. daily in summer; 11 A.M. to 4 P.M. daily in spring and autumn through Christmas. Hours vary January through March. Call for information.
Fees: $4 adults; $1.50 children 12–17; $1 children under 12
Facilities: Gift shop, gardens, and restrooms

Directions:
From the North: Take the Garden State Parkway south to Exit 6, turn onto Route 147, and proceed into North Wildwood, where the road becomes New Jersey Avenue. Stay on New Jersey Avenue until you come to Chestnut Avenue. Turn left onto Chestnut and go two blocks to Central Avenue. You'll see the lighthouse.

From the South: Take the Garden State Parkway to Exit 4 and turn right onto Rio Grande Avenue. Follow the signs to Wildwood. You'll cross over a drawbridge. Once in Wildwood, turn left onto Atlantic Avenue to 1st Avenue in North Wildwood. Turn left onto 1st Avenue and proceed to Central Avenue and turn right. The lighthouse is on Central Avenue near 1st Avenue.

Birdbath and house at the Hereford Inlet Lighthouse ➤

Hereford Inlet Lighthouse

In 1913, when beach erosion threatened the lighthouse's collapse, residents physically relocated it 150 feet west of its original location.

THE LIGHTHOUSE

The house itself has been restored and today looks as it did in Victorian times, with warm wallpaper and period furniture throughout. However, as cozy and charming as it is inside, its most compelling feature is its outdoor gardens.

Thanks to the painstaking and patient efforts of Steve Murray, North Wildwood's superintendent of parks, and a score of volunteers, the gardens have literally blossomed over the years into year-round seaside treasures.

Murray has had to nurse, cajole, and coax the garden over the years, and the effort has paid off in terms of stunning beauty. This was no small task, considering Murray had to import dirt to replenish the property's sparse dunes. At last count, the gardens harbored 46 perennials, 40 annuals, 18 varieties of shrubs, 11 types of vines, and numerous trees and ornamental grasses.

◀ *Garden at the Hereford Inlet Lighthouse*

To help other seaside gardeners, Murray has written a delightful and comprehensive booklet on his labor of love entitled *A Guide to the Hereford Inlet Lighthouse Gardens: With Tips and Observations for the Seashore Gardener*. Information about this little gem appears in Appendix B: Recommended Reading.

Because the lighthouse sat on an inlet, the 60-foot tower housed a small, fourth-order Fresnel lens.

TRAIL

A small path through the gardens leads to the beach.

TRIVIA

Laura Hedges was Hereford Inlet's only female lighthouse keeper, having assumed the role upon her husband's death in 1925.

27

Cape May Migratory Bird Refuge
Skimmers and Swimmers

OVERVIEW

For nature lovers, no trip to Cape May is complete without a visit to the Nature Conservancy's William D. and Jane C. Blair Jr. Cape May Migratory Bird Refuge. Known affectionately among birders simply as "The Meadows," the 212-acre refuge—co-managed by the Nature Conservancy and New Jersey Audubon Society—is a treasure trove for birders, wildflower enthusiasts, and anyone seeking a simple but hearty walk, in this case a mile-long stroll through meadows, marshes, and beaches.

The Meadows has something to offer no matter what time of the year you visit. Watch for raptors and shorebirds in the fall and spring; elusive yellow-crowned night herons and least bitterns in summer; and black ducks, Northern shovelers, and mergansers in winter.

In late May and early June, take particular care on the beach: This is the favorite nesting site for three endangered species: the piping plover, least tern, and black skimmer.

The Meadows is an excellent spot for nature photography. Shutterbugs can best shoot in the late afternoon or early evening, when the low sun casts a

Cape May Migratory Bird Refuge
212 acres
West Cape May Borough, Lower Township
Cape May County
Phone: (609) 861-0600 – Nature Conservancy's
Delaware Bayshore Center office in Delmont

Hours: Open daily dawn to dusk.
Fees: None, although a donation is suggested
Facilities: Observation deck is wheelchair
accessible.

Directions:
From all points: Once in Cape May, take Route 606 (Sunset Boulevard) toward Cape May Point. The parking lot will be on your left, just beyond the right-hand turn for Bayshore Road.

warm, golden glow over the area. However, don't eschew shooting after the sun settles behind the horizon. When conditions are right, the evening clouds take on the hues of glowing opals. Those colors, with Cape May Point Lighthouse in the background, will give you one nice postcard shot.

HISTORY

The refuge was actually once a meadow in the Victorian resort town called South Cape May. A coastal storm in the 1950s destroyed the town but the meadows remained, becoming the focal point for local grazing and recreation. The refuge was established in 1981.

TRAIL

The Meadows trail is really one large loop. As you head toward the beach, the trail takes you from the gravel parking lot on Sunset Boulevard through the

The Meadows

woods, past two ponds and an observation deck. Along the route, watch for several varieties of wildflowers, including field goldenrod and the rare collared dodder. In the ponds watch for bitterns and herons gazing out from the phragmites. Willets, greater and lesser yellowlegs, and great and snowy egrets can be seen in the ponds and marshes.

The trail proceeds up a sandy slope through secondary dunes and the beach. This is where you'll find your shorebirds, including sanderlings and ruddy turnstones, during the migration months. Again, be watchful for piping plovers, least terns, and black skimmers in late spring.

Turn left and walk until you reach the path that will return you to the refuge. A staircase will bring you back to the refuge's marshes and ponds. Eventually, the trail loops through a large meadow to the parking lot.

This is an easy trail, but those who walk with difficulty may find the dune slopes difficult to master, especially after a rain, when the wooden stairway becomes slippery. In that case, eschew the beach, double back down the trail, and take the loop in the opposite direction.

Observation platform at the Cape May Migratory Bird Refuge

Two other pieces of advice: First, poison ivy is profuse here, so pay attention to where you walk and where you stand. (This is a true story. My very first excursion into the Meadows was some years ago, on a morning walk led by noted New Jersey Audubon naturalist Pete Dunne. To help me get a better view of a least bittern, Pete planted my spotting scope in a lush bed of poison ivy. Somehow I managed not to come down with its annoying, itchy rash, and I got a great view of the bittern.)

Second, the trail can turn into one large puddle after heavy rains. Bring boots as a precaution, unless you want to tackle the puddles—with their profusion of Canada goose effluent—barefoot.

Birding at the Cape May Migratory Bird Refuge ➤

TRIVIA

Birders or not, visitors should be tuned in to one seasonal attraction. Every September thousands of migrating black skimmers skim the ponds for crustaceans and other treats. They then return to the beach to collectively rest and digest. It's an entertaining, not to mention educational, experience.

Black skimmer at the Cape May Migratory Bird Refuge

28

Cape May Point State Park
Where the Waters Meet

OVERVIEW

Cape May Point State Park sits at the very bottom of the Garden State, where the Atlantic Ocean meets the Delaware Bay. Like everywhere else in Cape May County, "The Point" is a birding hot spot, especially during the fall migration months, when thousands of raptors, shorebirds, and monarch butterflies soar down the eastern flyway on their voyage south.

It's also a great place to bring a picnic lunch, stroll quiet trails in the 153-acre Natural Area, hike the dizzying spiral staircase in the 157-foot tall lighthouse, fish, and bask in the warm beach sun.

Cape May Point endured a plague of soil erosion and invasive phragmites until the winter of 2005, when the U.S. Army Corps of Engineers engaged in a massive project that killed much of the invasive coastal weeds and extended the coastline by as much as 200 feet.

HISTORY

Originally called Sea Grove, The Point was settled in the mid-17th century by whalers from New York and New England. It became a popular Presbyterian summer retreat by the 1870s. The town's name was changed to Cape May Point in 1878.

Cape May Point State Park
235 acres
Lighthouse Avenue, West Cape May
Cape May County
Phone: (609) 884-2159 – Park;
(609) 884-5404 – Lighthouse
Web site: www.njparksandforests.org

Hours: The park is open daily from dawn to dusk. Lighthouse hours vary; call (609) 884-5404 for more information.
Fees: Park grounds are free; admission to the lighthouse is $5 adults, $1 for children 12 and under.
Facilities: Museum and museum shop, nature center, restrooms, picnic pavilions, and observation platform; handicap accessible

Directions:
From all points: Once in Cape May, follow Sunset Boulevard, also called Route 606, west toward Sunset Beach. Turn south at Lighthouse Avenue (there will be a sign). The park will be on your left.

Like other Jersey seaside towns, The Point rapidly became a favorite summer resort town in the early 1900s. During World War II the area was home to a coastal defense base and bunkers, built as part of the 1942 Harbor Defense Project.

The state acquired the land after the federal government decommissioned the base in 1963. The state park opened in 1974, retaining two of the base's buildings for use as the park office/visitor center and an Environmental Education Center.

Walking The Point ➤

THE LIGHTHOUSE

Built in 1859, the lighthouse you see today is the area's third (the other two were built in 1823 and 1847). Like its sister lighthouse at Barnegat [see #16], it was built by Army Lt. George Meade, and contained a first-order Fresnel lens. The last of the lighthouse keepers retired in the 1930s, after the light was automated. Today the lighthouse is listed on both the state and national registers of historic places.

Since 1986 the lighthouse has actually been leased to the Mid-Atlantic Center for the Arts, a nonprofit group in the Emlen Physick Estate in Cape May. The group has been restoring the lighthouse, bit by bit, for more than 10 years. Restoration work includes the windows, doors, lantern roof, and staircase. The lighthouse's original bathrooms and old walkways were also uncovered.

Tourists have been hiking the lighthouse's 199-step cast-iron spiral staircase since the late 19th century. Today more than 100,000 visitors annually take the climb.

Lighthouse at Cape May Point State Park

The sweaty palms and huffing and puffing are worth it: A view of the cape and surrounding waters awaits visitors at the top. Along the way, visitors can rest in window alcoves where they are treated to exhibits on area history as well as lighthouse building secrets.

Visitors favoring more grounded entertainment can visit the museum gift shop in the former oil house.

TRAILS AND SIGHTS

There are three trails in the park's Nature Area—the half-mile-long Red Trail, the 1.5-mile Yellow Trail, and the 2-mile Blue Trail. Very flat and easy to walk, they all start from a common entrance in the main parking lot.

The Nature Area is a great place to visit any time of the year. My favorite time, however, is early September. Monarch butterflies abound as they start their winter migration, teacup-sized white and pink swamp rose mallow is in bloom, and the trail is awash with the white petals and heady perfume of clematis, also called Virgin's bower.

Photographic opportunities abound on the trails, from shooting birds and butterflies to plants and wildflowers. Also be alert for shooting interesting angles of the lighthouse, since it can be viewed from some various vantage points.

RED TRAIL

The park's shortest trail is the easiest for the elderly and families with young children. The narrow boardwalk was recently replaced with a wider walk made of recycled plastic, making it easier to push strollers or to use walkers and canes.

The trail takes you through wetlands lined with phragmites and an assortment of plants and wildflowers, including eastern baccharis, trumpet creeper, poison ivy, and bugleweed. At the fork, turn left to stay on the trail; or if you prefer, continue straight onto the Yellow and Blue Trails.

A short detour off the Red Trail leads to an observation blind overlooking Lighthouse Pond. Here, watch for waders like egrets, great blue herons, and least bitterns. In late fall and winter, look for an assortment of ducks, including mallards, American wigeons, and ruddy ducks.

The trail continues to an observation deck overlooking another part of Lighthouse Pond. This is a good spot to watch for ospreys and bitterns. From here the trail takes you through an upland wood field with white oak, black gum, and common greenbrier. In late July and early August, watch for a profusion of Japanese honeysuckle.

From here the trail loops back to the parking lot. You can either return to the lot or take the Yellow and Blue Trails, which share the same route before splitting near the dunes.

YELLOW AND BLUE TRAILS

The 1.5-mile Yellow Trail and 2-mile Blue Trail lead visitors through a State Natural Area, which encompasses an assortment of freshwater marshes, upland woodlands, and sand dunes. The paths here are a combination of the park's older, natural wooden boardwalk and sandy paths.

Start your walk at the main trail entrance in the parking lot, and continue straight when the trail splits from the Red Trail. Soon after crossing a small bridge you'll come to the Natural Area. You'll pass phragmites, trumpet-vine, poison ivy, greenbrier, clematis, black cherry trees, and porcelain berry, a pretty but invasive vine-type bush that can reach a height of 16 feet.

The boardwalk becomes a sandy path as you proceed through the freshwater marshes. When in the marshes, try to walk quietly, because it's possible to come across egrets and herons striding close to the marsh edge as they hunt for food.

At one point the trail proceeds through a forest of mockernut hickory trees. According to an interpretive display, the tree can grow as tall as 120 feet. Indians used its fruit to treat colds.

A short detour from the trail leads to an observation deck overlooking Lighthouse Pond, where you can look for waders and ducks.

After this the trails split. The Yellow Trail leads through more wetlands and uplands to the dunes and the parking lot. The Blue Trail also proceeds through woodlands and marshlands to the dunes, but farther north.

If taking the Blue Trail in late spring, take particular note of the posted signs restricting dune access. The dunes are a prime nesting area for piping

◀ *Red Trail at Cape May Point State Park*

plovers, least terns, and black skimmers, and home to seabeach amaranth, an endangered seaside plant.

As you proceed toward the parking lot you'll pass Al's Pond, a very good place to watch for winter waterfowl migrants, like pintails and ruddy ducks. Overlooking the pond is the hawk-watch platform, home of New Jersey Audubon's annual hawk-watch count.

ENVIRONMENTAL EDUCATION CENTER

The park's Environmental Education Center provides visitors with an up-close and personal look at some of the reptilian and amphibian locals. Snug within their tanks, often staring back, the attractions include corn snakes and black rat snakes, diamondback terrapins, and two tiny gray tree frogs, a species on the state's endangered list.

"THE BUNKER"

One item of interest in the park is a World War II bunker that once served as part of the 1942 Harbor Defense Project. Now deserted, it's a large, impressive, and imposing mass. It was originally set back 900 feet from the shoreline, where erosion caused it to be half-buried at high tide. Thanks to the recent environmental restoration project, it's no longer submerged.

As an aside, the New Jersey coast—like the rest of the eastern seaboard—was well patrolled and protected during World War II. My father, John Sweeney, was part of that patrol before he was shipped to the Pacific Theater of Operations in 1945.

BIRDING GALORE

Because it sits so prominently on the Atlantic flyway, the park is a popular birding spot, especially during the fall migration when visitors from all over the world flock to New Jersey Audubon's hawk-watch platform to visually gorge on the parade of raptors.

Twilight tree at Cape May Point State Park ➤

The Point is also a great place to bird at other times of the year. From the park's seaside pavilions, you can watch for shorebirds and pelagics, or you can hike the Natural Area in search of waders, ducks, songbirds, and owls.

In spring you don't have to wander far to get a good look at seldom-seen species. Purple martin houses, designed like little apartment complexes, sit near the park office, giving visitors excellent views of their winged tenants.

TRIVIA

The lighthouse contains bricks from the second lighthouse that was built in 1847.

29

Higbee Beach Wildlife Management Area
Winging It with Warblers

OVERVIEW

Like "The Meadows" [see #27] and Cape May Point State Park [see #28], the 886-acre Higbee Beach Wildlife Management Area (WMA) is famous for the annual avian fall migration. If a cold front has moved through and the winds are right, you're almost guaranteed to experience a raptor fallout. One brisk morning I encountered numerous merlins, Cooper's hawks, sharp-shinned hawks, and American kestrels—all in just 30 minutes.

HISTORY

An old Cape May family, the Higbees, owned the property from 1793 to 1940. The state acquired it in 1977 in an effort to protect endangered and non-game wildlife and to spare the tract from turning into a campground. A New Jersey Audubon survey of migrant activity helped to fuel the acquisition.

TRAILS

Higbee's trails loop around fields and upland forests before ending at the beach. The trails are overgrown, so it's best to tick-proof yourself by wearing long-sleeve shirts and boots, and tucking your pants legs into your socks.

Higbee Beach Wildlife Management Area
886 acres
West Cape May, Cape May County
Phone: (609) 628-2103 – NJ Division of Fish
and Wildlife; (609) 884-2736 –
New Jersey Audubon's Northwood Center

Hours: Open daily from dawn to dusk
Fees: None
Facilities: Two observation decks, a portable "seat of ease" in the parking lot for the non-discriminating visitor, great views, and plenty of fresh air; upland and waterfowl hunting permitted in season

Directions:
From all points: At the end of the Garden State Parkway, follow Route 109 west to Route 9. Turn left onto Route 9 and proceed to the first traffic light, turning left onto Route 162 (Seashore Road). Turn right on Route 641 (New England Road) and proceed 2 miles to the end of the road and the Higbee parking lot.

An observation platform is an excellent perch for birding. In migration months look for vesper sparrows, warblers, wood thrushes, robins, and cedar waxwings—not to mention the many raptors that fly through.

Once at the beach, scope the shoreline for shorebirds, such as red knots and sanderlings, and pelagics, such as brown pelicans, jaegers, and petrels. Keep an eye on the ocean for whales and dolphins.

Before you reach the beach's primary parking area, there's a wide sand road on your right. A walk down here brings you past another observation plat-form. The road eventually takes you to a fishing jetty and the beach, where you can get a good look at the Cape May-Lewes Ferry on the other side of the inlet.

Trail to Higbee Beach ➤

Male yellow warbler

TRIVIA

Higbee's beach draws another type of flock: Nude sunbathers. The natur-
ist migration forces officials to close the beach every summer.

Sail a tall ship ... explore a fort's ramparts ... hike a king's "realm" ...

Part 4
Delsea Region

30

Cape May National Wildlife Refuge
Trekking the Woodcock Trail

OVERVIEW

Having feasted on the southern-most pleasures of Cape May County, the Coastal Heritage Trail continues north along the shores of Delaware Bay.

Although this area is rife with marshes, your first stop—the Woodcock Trail of the 10,000-acre Cape May National Wildlife Refuge—is buried in pristine flat woodlands bordering a residential area. According to state figures more than 317 bird species, 55 kinds of reptiles and amphibians, and more than 40 kinds of mammals can be found here.

The refuge's trails are perfect for visitors who would like to sample the area's flora and fauna in a brief day trip, or as a break while on the way to, or from, other Cape May destinations.

HISTORY

Founded in 1989, the Cape May National Wildlife Refuge is a relatively new addition to a national refuge system founded by Theodore Roosevelt in 1903.

Cape May National Wildlife Refuge
10,000 acres
24 Kimbles Beach Road
Cape May Courthouse, NJ 08210
Cape May County
Phone: (609) 463-0994 – Office

Hours: Refuge is open daily from dawn to dusk. The office is open from 8 A.M. to 4 P.M. Monday through Friday.
Fees: None
Facilities: Restroom and brochures in the office; a few wooden benches on the Woodcock Trail

Directions:
From the North: Take the Garden State Parkway south to Exit 10, and turn south on Route 9. Make a right onto Route 658 (Hand Avenue), and turn south onto Route 47. Turn left onto Kimbles Beach Road and follow the road to the office. To reach Woodcock Trail, turn right onto Route 47 and follow south to the trail, which will be on your right.

From the South: Follow Route 47 north to Kimbles Beach Road if you want to visit the refuge office, or turn left onto Woodcock Trail, which you will hit first.

TRAILS

The refuge is separated into two parts: The office area on Kimbles Beach Road and the Woodcock Trail, located in a housing development on Woodcock Trail, south of the refuge offices.

The 1.5-mile trail at the office leads visitors through marshes to the beach. The 1-mile Woodcock Trail loops through woodlands, including a shady bower

Arbor at the Cape May National Wildlife Refuge ➤

of hardwoods and pitch pine, and around several fields. Watch for bluebirds, Eastern towhees, and indigenous wildflowers like pokeweed, goldenrod, and Eastern baccharis, which blooms with yellowish flowers in September.

TRIVIA

You can tell a trail is rarely taken by the number of spider webs you walk into, and the Woodcock Trail is full of them. Annoying? Yes, but think altruistically. By clearing the webs, you're doing your fellow visitors a favor.

31

Cape May Bird Observatory
Monarchs and Hummers

OVERVIEW

Comparing the Cape May town of Goshen to its Biblical counterpart might be a stretch, but its freshwater wetlands and salt marshes are a naturalist's heaven. It's also home to New Jersey Audubon's 26-acre Cape May Bird Observatory Center for Education and Research.

Set along Sluice Creek, the center is one of the most popular attractions along the Coastal Heritage Trail. Why? For one thing, two of the world's most renowned naturalists, author and Program Director Pete Dunne and butterfly expert Patricia Sutton, are headquartered here. For another, the gardens of its Model Backyard Habitat annually attract hundreds of monarch butterflies and ruby-throated hummingbirds, making it a great place to bird and butterfly watch. The center also has one heck of a good store where you can buy anything from nature books to stuffed toys for the kids to high-end binoculars and spotting scopes.

HISTORY

New Jersey Audubon purchased the site in 1993. The center was dedicated in 1997.

**Cape May Bird Observatory,
Center for Education and Research**
26 acres
600 Route 47 North
Cape May Court House, NJ 08210
Cape May County
Phone: (609) 861-0700
Web site: www.njaudubon.org

Hours: Open daily 9 A.M. to 5 P.M.
Fees: None, but New Jersey Audubon would love to have you as a member. Membership benefits include discounts on center programs and equipment.
Facilities: Book and gift shop, an upstairs loft/gallery for photography and art exhibits; field trips and educational programs for children and adults

Directions:
From the Northeast: Take the Garden State Parkway south to Exit 13 and turn right. Proceed to the light and turn left onto Route 9 south. Turn right onto Route 646 until you reach Route 47. Turn right and proceed south for just over a mile and a half. The center will be on your right. *Alternate route:* Take the Garden State Parkway to Exit 10 and turn right. From there, proceed straight until you reach Route 47. Turn left onto the highway and proceed south. The center is about a mile down on your left.

From the Northwest: Follow Route 47 south through Goshen. The center will be on your left.

From the South: Take the Parkway north to Exit 4 and follow the Rio Grande ramp to Route 47 north. *Alternate route:* Take the Parkway north to Exit 10. Turn left at the exit and proceed straight until you reach Route 47. Turn left onto the highway and proceed about a mile to the center.

Monarch butterfly

TRAIL

Visitors can take a short loop trail through the gardens and fields to a marshy area where you can often spot egrets and great blue herons, and the occasional least bittern. Palm and Cape May warblers can be found in the brush along the loop.

TRIVIA

The ruby-throated hummingbird is the state's only hummingbird species. Named for the male's gorget of iridescent red, this thumb-sized, gutsy little creature has a high-pitched chatter and perpetual need to consume sugar to maintain its nonstop frenetic energy.

32

Dennis Creek Wildlife Management Area
Graves and Clapper Rails

OVERVIEW

Depending on the direction of the tide, Dennis Creek, for which the 6,147-acre Dennis Creek Wildlife Management Area (WMA) is named, can be heaven or hell to paddle. Paddling with the current is one thing; paddling against it is another, as I learned on my first kayak trip here several years ago. What's that line attributed to Conan the Barbarian, "That which does not kill us makes us stronger?"

TRAILS

Jake's Landing, as Dennis Creek is known, is a peaceful place to both bird and butterfly watch. There are no paths or nature trails, but you can walk the road and check out the conifer forest and marshes.

Another option is to paddle the creek, where you can get a wonderful, often close-up view of Northern harriers, ospreys, and herons.

Whether you're on land or water, watch for the clapper rail, a reclusive wader known for its distinct clucking. I've only seen clapper rails a few times in Cape May, and once was here at Dennis Creek. An immature clapper rail had become trapped in a wire fishing pot left near the boat launch. As several of us

Dennis Creek Wildlife Management Area
6,147 acres
Dennis Township, Cape May County
Phone: (856) 629-0090 – NJ Division of
Fish and Wildlife

Hours: Open daily from dawn to dusk
Fees: None
Facilities: Boat ramp, observation deck; fresh air, great view; mind the tides when paddling

Directions:
From the North: Take Route 55 south to Route 47 south to North Dennis in Dennis Township. Stay on Route 47 but watch for the intersection with Route 557. Jake's Landing Road is on your right, just a third of a mile past the intersection. Take that road straight to the end; the boat launch area is approximately 1.5 miles from the highway.

From the South: Take Route 47 north through Goshen and North Dennis to Jake's Landing Road. Turn left and proceed through the conifer forest to the creek.

worked to free it, Mom clapper rail emerged from the reeds, and clucked and paced in the bird-equivalent of anxious hand wringing. Eventually, the young bird was freed, and it scuttled back with Mom into the marshes.

If you do paddle here, familiarize yourself with the local tide schedule. You'll save yourself a lot of trouble.

Another piece of advice: Mid-summer is prime time for the small but voracious strawberry flies. One summer, they were so aggressive that I had to abandon my spotting scope and hide in my car.

Marshes at the Dennis Creek Wildlife Management Area

TRIVIA

There's a very small, very old cemetery on the road to Jake's Landing, enclosed by black iron fencing and located in the conifer forest. According to a small sign, the cemetery belongs to the Ludlam family and includes the resting place of Zilpah Smith Ludlam, 1767–1829, and son Reuben Ludlam, born March 8, 1805, and died December 11, 1823. Look for it on the right as you approach the landing.

33

Belleplain State Forest
King Nummy's Realm

OVERVIEW

Nestled amid some of the highest elevations of southern New Jersey, Belleplain State Forest is deceptive in size. Traversing the silver waters of 26-acre Lake Nummy, the surrounding woods—primarily comprised of oaks, pines, and Atlantic white cedars—give a feeling of closeness and intimacy. So it's rather astounding to learn that the forest has more than 40 miles of trails encompassed within 21,034 acres.

Because of its many offerings, Belleplain is a favorite summer vacation spot, but visitors shouldn't eschew it in the off-season. The lake concession stands may be closed and the aluminum canoes stacked like sardines, but the trails can be tackled, the interpretive nature center visited, and the overall sense of a wonderful peace enjoyed.

HISTORY

Belleplain, which straddles the border of Cape May and Cumberland counties, was established by the state in 1928 for watershed conservation, wildlife management, and timber production. Originally the lake was a privately owned cranberry bog. It was converted into a lake by members of the Civilian

Belleplain State Forest
21,034 acres
County Route 50, P.O. Box 450
Woodbine, NJ 08270 (Mailing Address)
Cape May and Cumberland counties
Phone: (609) 861-2404
Web site: www.state.nj.us/dep/parksand
forests/parks/belle.html

Hours: The forest is open daily from dawn to dusk. Between Memorial Day and Labor Day, the lake is open for swimming from 10 A.M. to 6 P.M.

Fees: Entrance fees charged Memorial Day weekend through Labor Day are $5 weekdays and $10 weekends. There's no charge for walk-ins and bicyclists. Camping and picnicking fees vary; for the most up-to-date fees, contact the park office or visit the Web site.

Facilities: Three locations (Meisle Field, CCC Camp, North Shore) include 275 campsites, five yurts, and 14 lean-tos; hiking, swimming, boating, horseback riding, cross-country skiing, snowmobiling; lake recreation area with beach, restrooms, concession stand, canoe rentals; boat launch (off Jake's Landing Road), nature center, group cabin, playground, picnic pavilion; athletic fields; fishing, hunting, and trapping.

Directions:

From the Northeast: Take the Garden State Parkway south to Exit 17 and take Route 9 north to Route 550. Turn onto Route 550 through Woodbine; follow forest signs.

From the Northwest: Take Route 49 south, continuing below Millville. Turn right onto Route 557 and proceed southeast. Turn right at the junction with Route 550 and follow signs to the park.

From the South: Take Route 47 or 347 north to Route 550 through Belleplain and follow signs to the park entrance.

Nummy's Lake in Belleplain State Forest

Conservation Corps (CCC) during the Great Depression. Today, visitors come to hike, bike, swim, camp, picnic, paddle, bird, and, in the winter, cross-country ski.

TRAILS

Belleplain offers two types of trails, non-motorized and motorized, covering a total of 40 miles.

NON-MOTORIZED TRAILS

You can walk yourself silly in Belleplain State Forest. Twelve non-motorized trails cover 17 miles, all of which can be used for hiking, horseback riding, mountain biking, and cross-country skiing.

The longest of these trails, the East Creek Trail, is 7.16-miles long, and runs from East Creek Pond off East Creek Mill Road, to the offices at the Lake Nummy recreation area.

The other non-motorized trails include:

- Ponds Trail, 2.2 miles: Runs from the parking area near Pickle Factory Pond on Delsea Drive (Route 47), then crosses the Turtle Walk motorized trail to East Creek Pond.

- Old Cape Trail, 1.67 miles: Runs from the parking area on Weatherby Road (Route 548) to the Cinder Trail Parking Area.

- Seashore Line Trail, 1.46 miles: Runs from Weatherby Road, crossing Hunters Mill Road.

- Goff's Folly Trail, 0.98 mile: Runs off Jake's Landing Road in the southernmost part of the forest.

- Tarkiln Bogs Trail, 0.90 mile: In the northeast corner of the forest, can be reached off the parking area that connects Old Cape Trail, John's Run Trail, and Cinder Trail.

- North Shore Trail, 0.72 mile: Runs around the north shore of Lake Nummy, above the lake's nature trails; connects to Mackay's Crossing Trail, which brings you out to Belleplain-Woodbine Road, and to Goosekill Trail, which will take you to the Yellow Nature Trail and Meisle Trail.

- Meisle Trail, 0.61 mile: On Meisle Road parking area, across the road from Lake Nummy; connects with Goosekill Trail, Yellow Nature Trail, and East Creek Trail.

- Eagle Fitness Trail, 0.28 mile: Southeast of Meisle Trail, across from the Meisle Field and CCC Camp sites; can be accessed from Frank's Road.

- Goosekill Trail, 0.28 mile: Off Belleplain-Woodbine Road across the road from the forest's office.

In addition, two nature trails near Lake Nummy are interpretive walks, each less than a half-mile long. The first, or White, trail starts north of the lake's beach area, then loops around the lake's north shore below the campsite. Marked places of interest include mountain laurel, Atlantic white cedar, blackgum and sweetgum trees, American holly, a cedar swamp, scenic vista, pitch pine, and bracken fern.

Trail in Belleplain State Forest

The second or Yellow trail is adjacent to the first trail. This is a somewhat shorter loop that traverses the lower part of the lake. Again, signs point visitors to various local flora, including pitch and Virginia pines, red maples, and white oaks.

MOTORIZED TRAILS

Fourteen of Belleplain's trails, covering 24 miles, are open to trucks and motorcycles. No all-terrain vehicles are permitted in the park. Snowmobiles may be used but only in designated areas. The motorized trails can be reached by Belleplain-Woodbine Road (Route 550).

Caution: None of the motorized trails are typical paved roads. They're rugged, steep in some places, and downright wet and muddy in others.

Motorized trails include:

- Seashore Line Trail, 5.77 miles: Can be picked up on the eastern side of Belleplain and the parking area off Belleplain-Woodbine Road.

- Old Cape Trail, 2.78 miles: Runs from the parking area connecting Cinder Trail, Old Cape Trail, and John's Run Trail.

- Duck Pond Trail, 2.01 miles: Can be accessed off Timber Swamp Road in the northwest section of the forest; connects with Sally's Pond Trail.

- Tom Field Trail, 1.90 miles: Runs from the northwest side of the East Creek Pond to Cedar Bridge Road.

- Kalker's Pond Road, 1.67 miles: Can be accessed off Joe Mason Road in northwest corner of the forest.

- Beaver Causeway Trail, 1.46 miles: Located in the bottom, or southern portion, of the forest off Jake's Landing Road.

- Turtle Walk Trail, 1.41 miles: Can be accessed off Route 47 near Eldora; connects to Tom Field Trail.

- Sally's Pond Trail, 1.35 miles: Connects with Duck Pond Trail and Seashore Line Trail in northwest section of the forest.

- Dundrea Trail, 1.23 miles: Can be accessed off Steelmantown Road in the forest.

- Narrows Road Trail, 1.14 miles: Can be accessed in northeast corner of forest from Belleplain Road (Route 605).

- John's Run Trail, 1.05 miles: In the northern part of the forest; can be accessed off the parking area connecting Old Cape Trail and Cinder Trail.

- Washington Trail, 0.83 mile: In the southern part of forest off Jake's Landing Road; connects with Beaver Causeway Trail; can be accessed from Route 47 just west of Dennisville.

- Champion Trail, 0.82 mile: Can be accessed off Belleplain-Woodbine Road in the Lake Nummy Recreation Area.

- Cinder Trail, 0.58 mile: Located at top of forest; can be accessed from the parking area connecting Old Cape Trail and John's Run Trail.

TRIVIA

Lake Nummy supposedly was named for King Nummy, the last Lenni-Lenape chieftain to live in the area.

34

Eldora Nature Preserve
Rare Moths and Spider Webs

OVERVIEW

According to the Nature Conservancy, the 201-acre Eldora Nature Preserve is the home to rare and endangered moths and butterflies, including the marble underwing moth, sad underwing moth, precious underwing moth, and the rare skipper.

Located on Route 47 in Eldora, the preserve can be visited either as its own day trip or as part of a trip to other Delsea and Cape May destinations. Its arboreal trails are particularly inviting in the fall, when the changing leaves provide beautiful photographic opportunities.

HISTORY

The property's farmhouse, built in 1872, is headquarters to the group's Delaware Bayshores Center. Entomologist C. Brooke Worth, who lived here from 1965 to 1981, donated the land to the New Jersey Conservation Foundation in 1981. In 1982 the Foundation turned it over to the Nature Conservancy.

TRAILS

The preserve's marked trails lead visitors through marshes, meadows, and woodlands: Watch for egrets, ospreys, and yellow-shafted flickers. In spring all

Eldora Nature Preserve
201 acres
2350 Route 47
Delmont, NJ 08314
Cape May County
Phone: (609) 861-0600

Hours: Trails open daily from dawn to dusk
Fees: None
Facilities: Nature center and gift shop

Directions:

From the Northeast: Take the Garden State Parkway south to Exit 25 and turn right at the end of the ramp. Cross Route 9 and take Route 631 west until you come to Route 47. Turn right onto Route 47 and stay on the route. The preserve will be on your right after you pass a gas station.

From the Northwest: Take Route 55 south to Route 47 south. Follow the highway. The preserve entrance will be the first left following West Creek.

From the South: Take Route 47 north. The preserve entrance will be on your right. If you cross West Creek, you've gone too far.

sorts of warblers can be found, including pine and prairie warblers, black-throated green and black-throated blue warblers, and Northern parulas.

TRIVIA

According to the Nature Conservancy the preserve is the first in the state established to harbor rare and protected moths.

Trail at Eldora Nature Preserve ➤

35

Dennis Township Wetland Restoration Site
Eagles and Osprey

OVERVIEW

More commonly known as "Stipson's Island," the Dennis Township Wetland Restoration Site is a great place to watch for bald eagles, ospreys, clapper rails, black skimmers, and marsh and seaside sparrows.

A boat ramp is also available for paddlers. As at Jake's Landing [see #32, Dennis Creek Wildlife Management Area], you'll want to mind the tide schedules.

HISTORY

The site, set along the silt-laden marshes of West Creek, was a salt-hay farm in the 1950s. PSE&G bought it in 1994 as part of its 32,000-acre Estuary Enhancement Program—an ecological mitigation project aimed at restoring the Delsea area ecology. In 1996 PSE&G got rid of the dikes and built a network of inlets and channels to restore the tidal flow. Today it's co-managed by the Nature Conservancy.

TRAILS

A short nature trail at the head of the island leads visitors through marshes to two observation blinds, where you can get a good look at osprey platforms.

Dennis Township Wetland Restoration Site
560 acres
Dennis Township, Cape May County
Phone: 1-888-MARSHES (888-627-7437)

Hours: Open daily from dawn to dusk
Fees: None
Facilities: Trail boardwalks are wheelchair accessible.

Directions:
From the Northeast: From the Garden State Parkway, turn right at the light for Exit 10A (the Parkway has become a local highway at this point) and proceed straight to Route 47. Turn right onto Route 47, and proceed north until you come to Stipson's Island Road, which will be marked by a small road sign on your left. The road will bring you to the island.

From the Northwest: Follow Route 47 south through Eldora and turn right onto Stipson's Island Road.

From the South: Follow Route 47 north; turn left onto Stipson's Island Road. Or, if you are coming north on the Parkway out of Cape May, turn left at Exit 10A.

Try to visit Stipson's Island during a fall day when the winds are blowing in off the coast. The winds tend to push in rare pelagics like black skimmers.

TRIVIA

As it happens, PSE&G's estuary program is good community relations, considering it owns two nuclear power plants farther north—the Salem and Hope Creek Nuclear Generating Stations in Lower Alloway Creek Township.

Snag forest at the Dennis Township Wetland Restoration Site

Maurice River Township Wetland Restoration Site
For the Birds—Really

OVERVIEW

A few miles north of Stipson's Island, the Maurice River Township Wetland Restoration Site, a 1,390-acre area, is another part of PSE&G's massive wetlands mitigation project. This is a good place for bird-watching, especially during the spring migration, when shorebirds like red knots visit by the thousands to eat the eggs laid by the horseshoe crabs.

HISTORY

Purchased by the utility company in 1994, the area was once diked for salt hay farming. PSE&G removed the dikes and created a series of inlets and channels to restore the local fish population.

TRAILS

There are no trails, but visitors can get a very good look at shorebirds, waders, and the occasional bald eagle from the elevated boardwalk and observation deck. Fishing and crabbing are also popular activities here.

The waters are easily accessible by two boat ramps, but remember that Delsea mantra if you're paddling: "Mind the tides, mind the tides. ..."

Maurice River Township Wetland Restoration Site
1,396 acres
Maurice River Township, Cumberland County
Phone: 1-888-MARSHES (888-627-7437)
Web site: www.pseg.com (click on "Environment")

Hours: Open daily from dawn to dusk
Fees: None
Facilities: Wheelchair-accessible observation plat-
form, elevated boardwalk, and two boat ramps

Directions:
From the Northeast: Take the Garden State Parkway south to Exit 10; turn right and stay on that road until you reach Route 47. Take Route 47 north, past Stipson's Island Road, to Route 616 (Glade Road) and turn left. Make another left onto Thompson's Beach Road. Follow the road until you come to the parking area.

From the Northwest: Follow Route 47 south to Route 616 and turn right. Proceed 1.5 miles to Thompson's Beach Road and follow to the parking area.

From the South: Take Route 47 north to Route 616 and turn left. Proceed 1.5 miles to Thompson's Beach Road and follow to the parking area.

TRIVIA

You know the saying, "This place is for the birds?" This one certainly is, judging by the healthy quantity of droppings decorating the observation deck. Not that you'll need an umbrella, but watch where you sit.

Seagulls hanging out at the Maurice River Township
Wetland Restoration Site

37

East Point Lighthouse
Still Standing After All These Years

OVERVIEW

Poised amid the dunes, the East Point Lighthouse literally makes a pretty picture. Artists and photographers have sung its praises in myriad works. Migrants appear to favor it, too: Watch for thousands of shorebirds in the spring and monarch butterflies in the fall.

HISTORY

Like the Hereford Inlet Lighthouse in North Wildwood [see #26], the East Point Lighthouse is one of the smallest lighthouses in the state. Built in 1849 it's the second-oldest lighthouse still standing in the Garden State (Sandy Hook is the oldest), and was originally known as the Maurice River Lighthouse.

Like Hereford, East Point was a fourth-order lighthouse, used to guide oyster schooners through the mouth of the Maurice River to Delaware Bay and back.

The lighthouse was decommissioned after World War II. The state purchased it from the federal government in 1955 because it made a good boat launch for the nearby Heislerville Wildlife Management Area [see #38].

A fire in 1971 destroyed most of the building, roof, and lantern room. Thanks to various state and federal grants over the years, however, the Maurice River Historical Society has rebuilt the structure and restored the interior.

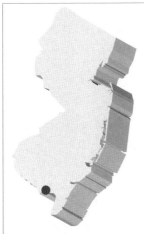

East Point Lighthouse
Heislerville, Cumberland County
Phone: (856) 327-5700

Hours: The lighthouse itself is open every third Sunday of the month from 1 P.M. to 4 P.M. April to October, and on the first Saturday in June from noon to 6 P.M. for Bay Day. The grounds, however, are open from dawn to dusk daily.
Fees: None
Facilities: Trail to the lighthouse, great views

Directions:
From the North: Follow Route 47 south to Route 616 (Glade Road) and follow to East Point Road. The road will take you straight to the lighthouse.

From the South: Follow Route 47 north to Route 616 (Glade Road) and follow directions above.

TRAILS

There are no formal trails, but you can beachcomb and bird-watch.

TRIVIA

Think your paycheck's small? The first lighthouse keeper, William Yarrington, was paid $250—a year. Custodians hired after the light was automated in 1905 were paid far less: One dollar a year. But there was a perk: They could live in the lighthouse rent-free.

East Point Lighthouse

38

Heislerville Wildlife Management Area
A Little "Brigantine"

OVERVIEW

Nestled between the Maurice River and Delaware Bay, the 5,134-acre Heislerville Wildlife Management Area (WMA) is, at least in my mind, a mini-Brigantine in terms of its beauty, migrants, and topography.

Like Brigantine the nature-viewing drive takes you over impoundments, salt-hay meadows, mud flats, and uplands, each harboring its specific avian residents and wildlife.

Snow geese in the thousands winter here. In spring, horseshoe crabs lay their eggs on the beaches.

TRAIL

Heislerville's trail is especially endearing to those who seek a passive-aggressive form of recreation. Towering phragmites make it impossible to see who's coming around the corner, and the pitted, sandy roads are so narrow that it's impossible for two vehicles to pass each other.

That said, Heislerville is one of my favorite spots in the region. The warm glow of a winter sunset favors its ponds and reeds, making it a photographer's delight, and the birding can be as bountiful as it is delightful.

Heislerville Wildlife Management Area
5,134 acres
Heislerville, Cumberland County
Phone: (856) 629-0090 – NJ Division of
Fish and Wildlife

Hours: Open daily from dawn to dusk
Fees: None
Facilities: Walking, birding, biking; deer, upland, and waterfowl hunting permitted in season.

Directions:

From the North: Follow Route 47 south and turn right onto Route 740 (Mackey's Lane). Turn left onto Route 616 (Dorchester-Heislerville Road), and travel 2.2 miles to Route 736 (Matt's Landing Road). From here, turn right and drive about 1 mile past the impoundments. There's parking on your left side, but you'll want to turn left at the sign marking the start of the driving route.

From the South: Take Route 47 north to Route 740 and follow directions above.

If you take the drive, simply follow the main road around the impoundments. You can't get lost, although you might feel anxious when you can't see beyond the reeds. There are some places to pull over for a better look at the ponds, but take care as fishing folk and crabbers use these nooks and crannies.

There's no law saying you can't walk this route, but I certainly wouldn't advise it.

Pond in the Heislerville Wildlife Management Area

TRIVIA

The spring horseshoe crab egg-laying attracts thousands of migrating shorebirds, not to mention an array of international visitors who come to view the spectacle.

39

Bayshore Discovery Project
Romancing the Schooner

OVERVIEW

Even landlubbers will find it hard not to love the sight of the *A. J. Meerwald*, New Jersey's official—and only—tall ship. With its three sails unfurled and engine cut, silently cruising into the Delaware Bay, the 115-foot long schooner invokes a romantic, long-lost past.

But if its appearance invokes romance, the *A. J. Meerwald* also recalls a time when life on the bay was as hard as it was lucrative. The schooner was just one of the hundreds that plied the bay waters at the height of the area's thriving oyster industry.

Although its harvesting days are gone, the *A. J. Meerwald* enjoys use as a floating classroom for the nonprofit Bayshore Discovery Project, annually hosting more than 15,000 passengers. In summer months, she serves as the project's roaming ambassador, putting in at ports like Burlington and Liberty Park. At other times she sails from her Bivalve port down the Maurice River out into the Delaware Bay.

The *A. J. Meerwald* may not be the project's only working schooner for long. At press time, volunteers were busy restoring the *Cashier*. Built in 1849 the 54-foot-long, two-masted schooner is said to be the oldest operational commercial vessel in the country.

Bayshore Discovery Project
2800 High Street
Port Norris, NJ 08349 (Mailing Address)
Cumberland County
Phone: (856) 785-2060
Web sites: www.ajmeerwald.org and
www.bayshorediscoveryproject.org

Hours: Wharf is open year-round. The museum is open from 1 P.M. to 4:30 P.M. weekends April through October. Call ahead for the *A. J. Meerwald* sailing schedule, as she is frequently visiting other Jersey ports in the spring and summer months.

Fees: None to visit the wharf; various ticket prices apply to a cruise aboard the *A. J. Meerwald.*

Facilities: Maritime museum complex; 115-foot-tall ship, the *A. J. Meerwald*; lectures, events, classes, boat-building shop, library, café, gallery, gift shops, and docks for visiting ships and boats

Directions:

From the North: From Route 55, take Route 47 south to Route 553. Turn south on High Street in Port Norris, and follow signs to Bivalve and the center. The project office is located at 2800 High Street. The museum is at 1727 Main Street in Port Norris.

From the South: Follow Route 47 north to Route 553 and follow directions above.

Flag off the stern of the A. J. Meerwald

HISTORY

Formerly called the Delaware Bay Schooner Project, the Bayshore Discovery Project has, since 1988, preserved the history and culture of the Delaware Bayshore while educating the public on its maritime heritage.

The project's center is in the town of Bivalve on the Maurice River. Founded in 1904 the town's wharves and shipping sheds once served as the center of the Delaware Bay's oyster industry, employing thousands until, in the 1950s, disease destroyed 90 percent of the oyster beds. Although the industry has revived somewhat, it has come nowhere near the strength of its golden days.

Today the town's shipping sheds and wharves, built by the Central Railroad Company in 1904, have been restored as an interpretive museum. They are listed on the National and State Registers of Historic Places.

Built in 1928 the *A. J. Meerwald* was a broken-down heap when local conservationists restored her and, in 1996, turned her into a floating classroom.

Foresail of the A. J. Meerwald ➤

Wharf at the Bayshore Discovery Project

She was designated the state's official tall ship by Gov. Christine Todd Whitman in 1998.

TRAILS

There are no trails to speak of, but visitors can park in the center parking lot and visit the interpretive exhibits lining the sheds and wharves.

You can also leave the car where it is and visit the PSE&G's Commercial Township Wetland Restoration Site [see #40], just across High Street, or walk or bike along the bicycle path that runs from the project's center through Port Norris; Al's Hideaway, on the road to Shellpile, is a fun bar and restaurant to visit.

TRIVIA

Oysters begin their lives as males, but later become females.

40

Commercial Township Wetland Restoration Site
More Fun in the Phragmites

OVERVIEW

Across the street from the Bayshore Discovery Project in Bivalve [see #39], the 4,200-acre Commercial Township Wetland Restoration Site is another salt-hay restoration project in PSE&G's Estuary Enhancement Program, co-managed by the Nature Conservancy. If you're coming off a sail on the *A. J. Meerwald*, a stroll along the site's boardwalk and nature trail will help you regain your land-legs.

HISTORY

In the 18th century, farmers built dikes in the wetlands to farm salt hay. After purchasing the property for its Estuary Enhancement Program in 1994, PSE&G removed the dikes and restored the inlets and channels necessary to maintain natural tidal flow.

TRAIL

The 4-mile nature trail (2 miles out, 2 miles back) offers visitors a great view of the Maurice River estuary. The marshes are particularly mysterious in a

Commercial Township Wetland Restoration Site
4,300 acres
High Street
Bivalve, Cumberland County
Phone: 1-888-MARSHES (888-627-7437)

Hours: Open daily from dawn to dusk
Fees: None
Facilities: Wheelchair-accessible trail, paved bike/hike/equestrian path, and parking lot

Directions:
From the North: From Route 55, take Route 47 south to Route 553. Turn south on High Street in Port Norris, and follow signs to Bivalve and the nature trail.

From the South: Follow Route 47 north to Route 553 and follow directions above.

thick, morning fog. As elsewhere along the coast, you'll get your fill of egrets, seagulls, and ospreys.

The trail starts with an elevated boardwalk on High Street. Turn right, and a brief detour will take you to an observation area where you can often see numerous shorebirds, including dunlin and sanderlings, and waders like great blue herons and egrets.

Returning to the main trail, continue for approximately 2 miles through the marshes and phragmites. The boardwalk becomes a paved path that ends at an observation platform. There's an osprey nest in the marshes; watch for osprey pairs and chicks in early June.

Marshes at the Commercial Township Wetland Restoration Site

You can also forego the walk and drive down High Street to the parking lot at the observation platform.

TRIVIA

Purple martin houses stand near the trail entrance. Watch for the birds during the April nesting season.

A great egret stands in the marshes at the Commercial Township Wetland Restoration Site

41

Egg Island Wildlife Management Area
Nature with a Bite

OVERVIEW

The 8,398-acre Egg Island Wildlife Management Area (WMA) is yet another great place to stretch your legs and enjoy nature. It's a gorgeous spot, filled with tidal creeks and an assortment of cedars, bayberry bushes, and phragmites.

Visitors can bird from the observation deck, hike the walking trails, or fish and crab from the footbridge. If you crab, visit in September, when the crustaceans are lusciously large and plump.

A trip to Egg Island WMA can be easily combined with visits to nearby Glades Wildlife Refuge [see #42]—in fact, Rybins Beach sits at the western tip of Egg Island—and Fortescue State Marina [see #43].

TRAILS

Like most wildlife management areas, the trails here are rustic; that is, they are often overgrown, slippery after hard rains, icy in winter, and extremely buggy. That said, if you're properly outfitted, you'll find its marshes and wetlands ripe with birding opportunities, since the ecology invites an assortment of species, from waders and shorebirds to raptors and waterfowl, throughout the year. Little blue herons and yellow-crowned night herons, Northern harriers,

Egg Island Wildlife Management Area
8,398 acres
Dividing Creek, Cumberland County
Phone: (856) 629-0090 – NJ Division of
Fish and Wildlife

Hours: Open daily from dawn to dusk
Fees: None
Facilities: Parking lot, observation deck, footbridge, nature trails for birding, crabbing, and fishing; boat launch; upland and waterfowl hunting permitted in season

Directions:
From all points: Take Route 533 to Dividing Creek and turn south onto Maple Street. The area is at the end of the road, approximately 2.7 miles from Maple Street. You will see the footbridge.

hooded and common mergansers, blue-winged teal, marsh sparrows, and greater and lesser yellowlegs are among the avian species you'll find here.

If you prefer, you can climb the observation tower near the footbridge. From here you can get an excellent view of the area uplands and wetlands: Watch for raptors during the fall migration months.

Boaters and paddlers can put in to Hansey's Creek near the observation tower, and then travel down the creek to the bay and around Egg Island itself. It gets very windy in this part of the state, so hang on to your hat. Also, mind the local tide charts. Adventurous boaters might want to travel east to East Point Lighthouse [see #37], or proceed west, then north around the island to Rybins Beach.

Bridge to Egg Island ➤

Both upland and waterfowl hunting are permitted here during the fall, winter, and spring hunting seasons. If you want to hunt here, follow state rules and regulations. If you don't hunt, don't hike the island for safety reasons unless you visit on a Sunday. The state prohibits hunting on Sunday.

TRIVIA

Egg Island is also known as "Turkey Point." How it got this name is unknown, although speculation is that at one time the area was known for a profusion of wild turkeys.

◀ *Marshes at Egg Island*

42

Glades Wildlife Refuge
Migrants and Mating Dances

OVERVIEW

Set along the Delaware Bay, Glades Wildlife Refuge, known as "The Glades," takes visitors on a trip through many habitats, including marshes, upland woods, and, finally, white—and windy—dunes. This is a popular haven for snow geese in winter and shorebirds in spring.

A trip to the refuge can be combined with a visit to Egg Island Wildlife Management Area [see #41] and Fortescue State Marina [see #43].

The refuge has been part of the Natural Lands Trust inventory since 1963.

TRAILS

There are four parts to the The Glades. Three areas—Russell Farm and the Fortescue and Rybins beaches—are opened daily to the public. The fourth, the Reineman Wildlife Sanctuary, can be accessed by appointment only; try to visit in May, when the sanctuary is awash in blooming mountain laurel.

The Russell Farm Trail takes visitors on a walk through swamps and woods to a tidal marsh and observation tower, where you can watch for waders, raptors, and warblers. If you visit during the springtime mating season, you may be able to hear, if not see, the elusive black rail. But do be warned: The trail is

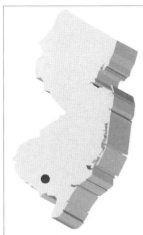

Glades Wildlife Refuge
Downe Township, Cumberland County
Phone: (856) 447-3425

Hours: Open daily from dawn to dusk
Fees: None
Facilities: Interpretive beach trail; parking at Russell Farm Trail and along seawall outside Fortescue

Directions:
From all points: At Route 553 in Newport, turn south onto Route 656 and proceed to the blinking yellow light. Turn south on Route 637 and follow the signs into Fortescue. Parking for Russell Farm Trail is 2.4 miles on your left from the Newport blinker. *Note:* Take care! You'll miss the entrance because it's unmarked. If it's the beach trail you're after, then continue through Fortescue and turn left on New Jersey Avenue. Continue to the end of the seawall and park. If going to Turkey Point, take Route 553 toward Dividing Creek; bear right at Turkey Point Road.

usually overgrown with weeds and phragmites. Wear boots after heavy rains and always use insect repellent for mosquitoes, ticks, and flies.

If you prefer an easier walk, then take the trails at the Fortescue and Rybins beaches on the Delaware Bay. Both are excellent spots to watch the spring shorebird migration, when thousands of shorebirds on their way home from wintering in southern climes pause to eat horseshoe crab eggs.

Visitors don't have to walk anywhere to enjoy one of the refuge's annual events. In early spring, the mating ritual of the male woodcock can be viewed roadside. The ritual is a curious affair, highlighted by a repetitive call similar to the sound of a high-pitched whoopee cushion. This noise precedes a frenetic,

Dunes at the Glades Wildlife Refuge

spiraling flight by the male, who quickly descends to where he started. If no female responds, he repeats the performance. To some, this may suggest a high school dance with wings.

TRIVIA

The refuge supports more than 200 species of ferns and flowering plants, including pond pine and mistletoe.

43

Fortescue State Marina
"Weakfish Capital of the World"

OVERVIEW

The town of Fortescue in Downe Township still calls itself the "Weakfish Capital of the World," due to a once thriving weakfish industry. Fortescue State Marina was once a part of that era, which is celebrated annually by a local weakfish fishing tournament. It's still a busy marina, used mainly by charter fishing boats.

The vessels, along with the cormorants, egrets, and seagulls that loiter along the pier, make for engaging photographs.

Combine your visit to Fortescue State Marina with trips to the Egg Island Wildlife Management Area [see #41] and the Glades Wildlife Refuge [see #42].

HISTORY

Downe Township was once the tourism center of southern New Jersey. Storms in the last century destroyed hotels and homes and the visitors have declined, but the area still has a thriving charter fishing boat industry, and the bayside summer business continues to be strong.

The marina, which continues to berth charters, is a throwback to that era. It was purchased by the state in the mid-1930s. Today it's managed by the Fortescue Captains and Boat Owners Association.

Fortescue State Marina
Fortescue, Cumberland County
Phone: (856) 447-5115

Hours: Open daily from dawn to dusk
Fees: Call for fees
Facilities: 125 slips for vessels up to 50 feet in length; ice, bait, and tackle available; restaurant, repair facilities, and interpretive exhibit outside office

Directions:
From all points: Take routes 553 and 656 to Newport and continue south on Route 637 to Fortescue. The marina will be on your right. If you miss the entrance, take the next right and follow the road. You'll eventually encounter the marina on your left. The marina office will be on your right.

TRAILS

There are no formal trails, although visitors can walk a dockside path to simply enjoy the ambiance and view the interpretive display that stands outside the association office.

TRIVIA

The weakfish, a sea trout, has been New Jersey's official fish since 1981.

Slips at Fortescue State Marina

44

Peaslee Wildlife Management Area
"Lost" in the Wilderness

OVERVIEW

One word sums up the Peaslee Wildlife Management Area (WMA): immense. Poised along the Tuckahoe River, approximately 7 miles southeast of Millville in Cumberland County, the 25,712-acre area can trick first-time visitors into thinking they are lost.

In a sense, they *are* lost—from the frazzles of everyday life. Peaslee's bogs and pine oak forests are sublimely peaceful and beautiful, particularly on an early-summer morning. Shafts of sunlight pour through the trees and the quiet air is rich with the smell of earth and pine. Indeed, the best things in life are free.

HISTORY

Peaslee is named for Amos J. Peaslee (1887–1969), an attorney who was a sometime delegate to the Republican National Convention and served as U.S. Ambassador to Australia. In fact, the state bought the area's first 8,847 acres from Peaslee in 1956. The area had originally been used for timber harvesting in the 1930s.

Peaslee Wildlife Management Area
25,712 acres
Millville, Cumberland County
Phone: (856) 629-0090 – NJ Division of
Fish and Wildlife

Hours: Open daily from dawn to dusk
Fees: None
Facilities: An interpretive sign at the main entrance
on Route 644 (Hesstown Road); birding and fishing; licensed hunters can hunt deer, upland fowl,
turkey, and waterfowl.

Directions:

From the North: Take Route 55 south from Vineland to Exit 24 and proceed
on Route 49 east to Route 644 (Hesstown Road). At Hesstown Road (look
for it carefully—it's marked by a small sign on your left), turn left and proceed 1.7 miles. Watch for a sand road on your left; that will take you on a
1.6-mile auto-tour loop.

From the South: Take 47 north from the Goshen area to Route 55 to Exit 24
and follow directions above.

TRAIL

Visitors can hike or drive Peaslee's woods and dirt roads. If you do proceed on foot, however, carry a Global Positioning System, since the way can
be confusing.

Otherwise, the 1.6-mile unpaved loop driving trail makes for a splendid
drive, as it takes you through an assortment of upland areas, cranberry and
cedar bogs, and a clover-filled pasture, all canopied with lush hardwoods and
pines. Watch for migrating hawks in fall and warblers in spring.

Because of its dense forests, photographers should consider using a flash, using high-speed film (400 to 800 ASA), or setting their digital cameras on a high ASA setting (400 to 800).

Be alert: The road's not marked, and there are smaller roads that branch off like tree limbs.

TRIVIA

The Peaslee WMA is part of the state's massive Pinelands National Reserve, a 1-million-acre portion of southern New Jersey encompassing seven counties. Established by Congress in 1978 the reserve is rich in significant resources, not to mention the habitat of more than 1,000 plant and animal species, 100 of which are endangered.

Road in the Peaslee Wildlife Management Area ➤

45

Manumuskin River Preserve
Haven for Rare Plants

OVERVIEW

Deep in the middle of Cumberland County, along the banks of the Manumuskin River, the 3,503-acre Manumuskin River Preserve is celebrated as much for its sense of remoteness—you can hear, but not see, the traffic from nearby Route 55—as for its scenic beauty. Because of its location off Route 47, a visit to the preserve can be easily combined with one to the Eldora Nature Preserve [see #34].

The trail takes you on a fascinating journey through various ecosystems, including mudflats, upland forests, and Atlantic white cedar swamps. Wear boots if there's been a good amount of rain. Insect repellent must be used to ward off mosquitoes, ticks, and flies.

HISTORY

Manumuskin Preserve housed a historic mill settlement in the late-18th century. An earthen dam allowed farming until tidal flooding destroyed the dam in 1889. The Nature Conservancy acquired the property in 1982.

Manumuskin River Preserve
3,503 acres
Intersection of Routes 47 and 55
Port Elizabeth, Cumberland County
Phone: (609) 861-0600

Hours: Open daily from dawn to dusk
Fees: None
Facilities: Nature trail for walking; horseback riding and dog walking permitted on designated trails; camping, hunting, bicycles, and motorized vehicles all prohibited. *Note:* Do not remove or disturb any plants.

Directions:

From the Northwest: Take Route 55 south to Exit 21, which is Schooner Landing Road. Turn left at the stop sign and follow the road to the gate at the end.

From the Northeast: Take the Garden State Parkway south to Exit 25 and turn right. Cross Route 9 and continue on Route 631 to Route 50. Turn right and proceed north on Route 50 to Tuckahoe. From Tuckahoe, turn left onto Route 49 and continue west to Route 55. Take Route 55 south to Schooner Landing Road.

From the Southwest: This is a little trickier. Take Route 47 north through Port Elizabeth to Schooner Landing Road on your right. You must follow the jughandle to stay on Route 47; you don't want to get swallowed up by Route 55. Once on Schooner Landing Road follow directions above.

TRAIL

The nature trail starts just outside a chain-link fence at the end of Schooner Landing Road. It's narrow and can be overgrown and muddy, thanks to a profusion of upland thickets and low-lying swamps.

A number of grist and sawmill communities were founded along the Manumuskin in the early-18th century. On your walk you'll see the ruins of the Fries Mill settlement, circa 1790.

Also, watch for the more than 30 rare plants that can be found on the preserve. These include Pine Barrens boneset, which blooms in wet bogs August to September, and stiff tick-trefoil.

The rare pine snake and the corn snake, along with two rare butterflies, the rare skipper and the dotted skipper, also inhabit the preserve.

TRIVIA

The Manumuskin River is a tributary of the Maurice River, which eventually feeds into the Delaware Bay.

Trail in the Manumuskin River Preserve ➤

46

Peek Preserve
Urban Pleasureland

OVERVIEW

On the fringes of downtown Millville, on the banks of the Maurice River, the 252-acre Harold N. Peek Preserve is one of those tranquil, unexpected pleasures one sometimes finds in a bustling urban area. Meandering along its trails, visitors can feel very much on holiday from the hectic world.

HISTORY

The preserve is named for Harold N. Peek, a commercial fisherman who lived on the property with his family from 1957 to 1992, when Natural Lands Trust, an environmental group headquartered in Media, Pennsylvania, purchased the property.

Jenkins Landing is named for Trust founder Allston Jenkins.

TRAILS

The three, short trails are all fairly steep in some places, so you may want to bring walking shoes or boots with good traction, or carry a walking stick.

The 1.5-mile Red Cedar Overlook passes through a white cedar swamp along a narrow, winding path overlooking the silver Maurice River.

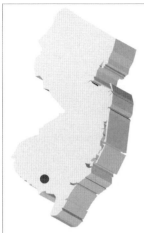

Peek Preserve
252 acres
P.O. Box 436, Newport, NJ 08345
(Mailing Address)
Millville, Cumberland County
Phone: (609) 447-3425 – Natural Lands
Trust field office, Newport

Hours: Open daily from dawn to dusk
Fees: None
Facilities: Parking and nature trails

Directions:
From the North: Take Route 47 south through Millville for 1.5 miles. Parking will be on your right, across from a housing development. The green sign is hard to spot, so be careful.

From the South: Take Route 47 north and stay on Route 47 as you come to the Route 55 jughandle. The preserve will be 3.5 miles from here; look for it on your left.

The 0.66-mile River Overlook Trail likewise loops around the preserve along the river through a mix of pine barrens, Virginia pine, and upland forests filled with chestnut and oak trees.

The shortest trail, the 0.5-mile Jenkins Landing Trail, brings visitors on a loop through woods to the river and back. An observation platform sits at the end of the boardwalk, where visitors can watch for waders, ospreys, and the occasional bald eagle.

TRIVIA

The wild rice here can grow as high as 7 feet in September.

Road in Peek Preserve

47

Green Swamp Nature Area
Cohansey River Enchantment

OVERVIEW

Like all the other sites in PSE&G's Estuary Enhancement Program, the 530-acre Green Swamp Nature Area encompasses wetlands and coastal salt marshes that are home to many bird species, including bald eagles, Northern harriers, ospreys, and waders like the great blue heron.

Besides enjoying a small nature trail, paddlers can put into the Cohansey River at a ramp off Back Neck Road.

Paddling east on the Cohansey will give boaters a bird's eye view of Brown's Run's osprey platforms, waders, and other birds.

HISTORY

Green Swamp Nature Trail has been part of PSE&G's wetlands mitigation project since the mid-1990s.

TRAIL

Green Swamp's 0.5-mile nature loop starts from the right side of the parking lot. The trail proceeds through a forested area to an observation site, where

Green Swamp Nature Area
530 acres
Fairfield Township, Cumberland County
Phone: 1-888-MARSHES (888-627-7437)

Hours: Open daily from dawn to dusk
Fees: None
Facilities: Parking, boat launch, observation area, nature trail, and classroom areas

Directions:

From the North: Take the New Jersey Turnpike to Exit 1 and the Deepwater Ramp. Turn right at the end of the ramp and continue straight to Route 130. Turn left on Route 130 and proceed through Pennsville. Turn onto Route 49 and proceed through Salem into Bridgeton. At Bridgeton, proceed south on 609 to Fairton. At Fairton, pick up Route 601, locally called Back Neck Road. Parking will be on your right about 2 miles down the road.

From the South: From the Millville area, take Route 49 north to Bridgeton and follow directions above.

Note: The Green Swamp Nature Area is one of those "you can't get there from here" places. If you wish to proceed north on the New Jersey Coastal Heritage Trail to the Greenwich Tea Burning Monument [see #48], you must return to Bridgeton and pick up Route 607 west. Route 607 will bring you into Greenwich and Ye Greate Street. Turn left onto Ye Greate Street. The monument will be on your right at the very next corner.

Boat ramp to the Cohansey River in the Green Swamp Nature Area

you can watch the osprey platform, then along a small boardwalk, from which you can get a glimpse of the broad Cohansey River and boat ramp before turning toward the parking lot.

Visitors can also stroll down the road to the boat ramp and river.

TRIVIA

Green Swamp is only one-half of PSE&G's 1,055-acre Cohansey River Wetland Restoration Site. The other half is the 525-acre Brown's Run Area in Hopewell Township.

48

Greenwich Tea Burning Monument
The Last Tea Party

OVERVIEW

South Jersey is rife with strange but true Revolutionary War tales. Erected in 1908 by the Cumberland County Historical Society, the Greenwich Tea Burning Monument marks the site of the state's only—and the nation's last—colonial protest involving tea. You might want to combine your visit here with one to the Hancock House State Historic Site in nearby Hancock's Bridge [see #50].

HISTORY

Staged in protest of British taxes, so-called "tea parties" had become popular in the pre-Revolutionary war colonies. The first occurred in Boston on December 16, 1773. Another was staged by the "New York Mohawks" in New York the following March. Boston "Indians" repeated the protest soon afterward.

Those protesters had merely heaved the shipments overboard, but in October 1774, a crowd in Annapolis forced one hapless importer to burn his own tea-laden ship.

Such was the volatile mood of certain colonials when, in December 1774, the *Greyhound*, a British brig commanded by one Captain Allen, stopped in

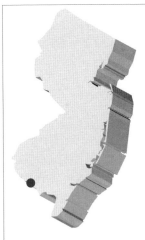

Greenwich Tea Burning Monument
Ye Greate Street
Greenwich, Cumberland County
Phone: (856) 455-4055 –
Cumberland Historical Society

Hours: Daylight hours only
Fees: None
Facilities: Roadside parking. Since the monument is downtown, however, it would behoove visitors to take a walking tour.

Directions:
From the North: Take the New Jersey Turnpike south to Exit 1 and the Deepwater Ramp. Turn right at the end of the ramp and proceed across the Route 294 overpass. Turn left onto Route 130 and proceed through Pennsville. The route turns into Route 49. Follow Route 49 south to Route 647. Take Route 647 west to Gum Tree Corner and turn onto Route 623 south. Route 623 becomes Ye Greate Street in Greenwich. The monument will be on your right in the center of town.

From the South: Take Route 47 north to Millville. From there, take Route 49 north to Bridgeton to Route 607 and turn left onto Ye Greate Street in Greenwich. The monument will be on the first corner on your right.

Cape Lewes, Delaware, while en route to Philadelphia. Tipped off that the Annapolis tea burning had riled up the locals, Allen sailed up the Cohansey to Greenwich, where he hid his tea shipment in the home of Loyalist Daniel Bowen. Unfortunately, the activity wasn't as secret as Allen would have liked. Several residents took note and investigated.

Greenwich residents were no newcomers to protesting British taxes, having held various protests since 1714. So it was that, on December 22, some 40 enthusiastic young men broke into Bowen's home, lugged the tea chests to a nearby field, and burned the entire stash.

The following year the first shots of the revolution rang out in Massachusetts. The colonials stopped burning tea and raised militia instead.

TRAILS

There are no formal trails, as the monument is downtown at the corner of Ye Greate Street and Delaware Avenue. But it would be a pity not to stop and visit this small historic town, founded in 1684. Many of the town's 18th- and 19th-century public and private buildings have been preserved, and there are tours available.

The Cumberland County Prehistorical Museum, at 1461 Bridgeton Road, contains an interesting collection of more than 1,000 fossils, an 800-year-old figure of a dog and her pups, and artifacts used by the post-Ice Age Indians who lived in the area.

TRIVIA

Loyalist officials, including Gov. William Franklin, Ben Franklin's illegitimate son, twice brought the Greenwich tea burners to trial. Both times jurors found "no cause for action," and the men were never convicted. Two of the tea burners, Richard Howell and Joseph Bloomfield, went on to serve as state governor.

Greenwich Tea Burning Monument

49

Stow Creek Viewing Area
Where Eagles Nest

OVERVIEW

Overlooking the Stow Creek estuary, the Stow Creek Viewing Area is one of the best places in New Jersey to experience the state's efforts to revive a once-dwindling bald eagle population. Pack your spotting scope if you want a good look at the eagles that call this small and quiet haven home.

The viewing area makes a pleasant stop between the Greenwich Tea Burning Monument [see #48] and Hancock House State Historic Site [see #50].

TRAIL

Hiking to the creek's observation platform is relatively easy, even in winter. The path leading to the observation platform and the creek is flat, except for the final, gentle slope leading to the platform. Wear boots after a hard rain, and sturdy hiking shoes—even crampons—in icy winter weather. Otherwise, hiking shoes, sneakers, or sandals are appropriate footwear.

Park your car (on the road, if you visit in winter, as the parking area is often unplowed), and follow the path to the T-intersection. There, you can turn left and make your way around the creek. Or, you can turn right and go to the observation platform.

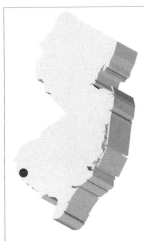

Stow Creek Viewing Area
Canton, Salem County
Phone: (609) 628-2103 – NJ Division of
Fish and Wildlife

Hours: Open daily from dawn to dusk
Facilities: Viewing platform, access road, parking
area, and interpretive exhibits

Directions:

From the North: Take the New Jersey Turnpike south all the way to Exit 1 and the Deepwater ramp. At the end of the ramp, turn right and proceed over the Route 295 overpass. Turn left onto Route 130, which turns into Route 49. In Salem, turn right at the sign for Hancock's Bridge, and turn left onto Route 658 (Hancock's Bridge Road). Turn right onto Route 623 (New Bridge Road) and head toward Canton. Parking for the viewing area will be 8 miles down on the right just before Stow Creek. If you cross the creek's bridge, you've gone too far.

From the South: From Millville take Route 49 north through Shiloh and turn south on Route 647. Follow into Gum Tree Corner and then head north toward Canton on Route 623 and follow directions above.

Getting to the platform can be somewhat confusing. There's a private farm to the right of the path, and as you proceed up the small slope, you may have the sense you're in the wrong place and are trespassing. Forget that sensation. At the top of the slope, to your left, is the platform, which gives you a good view across the wide creek.

Stow Creek as seen from the viewing platform

Stow Creek is another excellent place to watch for waders throughout the year and migrant ducks in late fall and winter.

TRIVIA

Did you know that Ben Franklin, one our country's formidable founding fathers, wanted Congress to name the wild turkey our national bird? Congress ignored the request and, instead, chose the more majestic eagle for that honor.

50

Hancock House
State Historic Site
Slaughter without a Shot

OVERVIEW

This modest brick home, set beside the quiet, phragmite-laden waters of Alloway's Creek, went down in the annals of state history as the site of a gruesome Revolutionary War massacre that occurred in the predawn hours of March 21, 1778.

HISTORY

THE MASSACRE

The winter of 1777–1778 was particularly trying for both armies in the Revolutionary War. Frozen and starving in the encampment at Valley Forge, Pennsylvania, General George Washington dispatched General "Mad" Anthony Wayne across the Delaware River in search of food, cattle, and horses. Wayne's raid was successful despite the area being populated with British troops, local Tory sympathizers, and neutral Quakers.

Not to be outmaneuvered, General Sir William Howe, whose troops had occupied Philadelphia since the previous October, ordered a similar raid in March. About 1,500 British troops under the command of General Charles Mawhood were dispatched to the same area Wayne had raided.

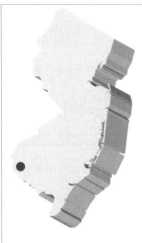

Hancock House State Historic Site
Hancock's Bridge, Salem County
Phone: (856) 935-3218

Hours: The grounds are open year-round from dawn to dusk. The house is open 10 A.M. to 4 P.M. daily Memorial Day through Labor Day; each first and third Saturday other times of year, or by appointment.
Fees: Donation requested
Facilities: Museum, parking, and tours

Directions:

From the North: Take the New Jersey Turnpike to Exit 1 and take the Deepwater ramp. Turn right onto the road at the bottom of the ramp, cross the Route 295 overpass, and turn left at Route 130. Route 130 turns into Route 49; follow it through Pennsville and Salem. Turn right at the sign for Hancock's Bridge, then turn left onto Route 658 and continue to the house.

From the South: From Millville, follow Route 49 to Route 667, and proceed west to Route 658, just before Hancock's Bridge.

The trouble was Mawhood's men ran into resistance from the local militia, and were soundly defeated in a skirmish. To teach the locals a lesson, Mawhood ordered his men to "spare no one. Put all to death: Give no quarters."

They didn't. Learning that 30 members of the militia were hiding in a home owned by Judge William Hancock, 300 British troops, under the command of Major John Graves Simcoe, stormed the house in the predawn sleet of March 21. The Redcoats bayoneted everyone, including Hancock and members of his family.

Not a single shot was fired. Ten colonials, including Hancock, were killed.

Believing more militia had bivouacked in the house, the British had hoped the attack would effectively disable the revolt in Salem County. It didn't, and the embarrassed British left the county within the week.

Today the massacre is commemorated at the house every March. There are history demonstrations, and a modified reenactment that includes an outdoor musket skirmish between Redcoats and patriots.

The house is open to the public on a regular basis, with one exception. For safety reasons the attic, which reportedly contains bloodstains from the massacre, is closed to visitors.

Reenactors at Hancock House

THE HOUSE AND PROPERTY

Another William Hancock initially purchased the land on which the house sits in 1675 from John Fenwick, an English Quaker who established the first permanent English settlement in what was then West Jersey.

Hancock willed the property to his nephew John who, in 1708, built a small bridge across the nearby creek. Hancock's Bridge, as it came to be called, played a prominent role in the area's commercial growth.

Hancock House

Judge Hancock's father, William, built the home in 1734, and its special feature is an end wall bearing what is called an "English Quaker" herringbone pattern of blue brick. Above the pattern, also in blue brick, is an "H" for Hancock, "W" for William, "S" for Hancock's wife, Sarah, and "1734," to mark the year the house was built. The house and property remained in the Hancock family until 1911. The state bought the house in 1931 for $4,000.

How the Hancocks used the house throughout the years remains unclear. According to local legal documents, it might have served as a tavern or hotel from 1761 to 1870.

TRAILS

There are no trails. The Hancock House is surrounded by a modest residential area.

A rampart overlooking the creek gives visitors a view of PSE&G's Alloway Creek Watershed Wetland Restoration Site [see #51]. This is a good place to watch for waders and ducks in winter and migrant songbirds in spring and autumn.

TRIVIA

Three documents, signed by Judge Hancock and on display in the house, were almost thrown out when county offices were renovated in the early 1970s.

Loyalist guard at the Hancock House

51

Alloway Creek Watershed Wetland Restoration Site
Birding in the Nuclear Age

OVERVIEW

The 2,900 acres of wetlands and uplands of the Alloway Creek Watershed Wetland Restoration Site comprise the most northern part of PSE&G's Estuary Enhancement Program (EEP). It is co-managed by the Nature Conservancy.

HISTORY

In the early 17th century, settlers diked the local wetlands so they could farm salt hay. They also built a fort, Fort Elfsborg, which lives on as the name of a local road. Today the area's primary industries are small dairy and produce farms, commercial businesses, and PSE&G's Salem and Hope Creek nuclear power plants.

TRAILS

Like PSE&G's other sites in its EEP, this one offers visitors the opportunity to bird, hunt, or simply enjoy a nature trail.

A short nature loop leads visitors to an observation blind and platform, where an assortment of species can be seen, depending on the season. This is a

Alloway Creek Watershed Wetland Restoration Site
2,900 acres
Lower Alloway Creek Township, Salem County
Phone: 1-888-MARSHES (888-627-7437)
Web site: www.pseg.com

Hours: Open daily from dawn to dusk
Fees: None
Facilities: Observation platforms, viewing blind, nature trail, and parking area

Directions:

From the North: To reach the Money Island Road parking area, proceed south on Route 49 from Salem to Route 658 and proceed southwest for about 2 miles. Turn right onto Fort Elfsborg Road, left onto Money Island Road, and take Money Island Road to the end. To reach the viewing area on Ft. Elfsborg-Salem Road, take Route 49 south through Salem to Route 625 (Chestnut Street) west. The name of Chestnut Street changes to Ft. Elfsborg-Salem Road; parking is at the end of the road. There's also a viewing area at the Hancock House [see #50].

From the South: To reach the Money Island Road parking area, take Route 49 north from Millville beyond Shiloh to Route 667 and proceed west to Route 623. Pick up Route 658 on the north side of Hancock's Bridge and follow directions above. To reach the viewing area on Ft. Elfsborg-Salem Road, continue on Route 49 until you reach Route 625 (Chestnut Street) west. Follow directions above.

Nature trail at the Alloway Creek Watershed Wetland Restoration Site

great site for spring migratory birding; be on the lookout for thousands of shorebirds, including dunlin, sanderlings, and ruddy turnstones.

A winter visit can be equally rewarding. Green-winged teal and hooded mergansers are plentiful, and the frosty-tipped phragmites that sparkle in the early morning sunlight have their own austere beauty.

There are three viewing areas. The primary area is on Money Island Road, where there's a parking area and trail loop that leads to an observation blind and platform. The second viewing area is on Ft. Elfsborg-Salem Road; the third, adjacent to the Hancock House State Historic Site [see #50].

The area is literally situated on Alloway's Creek and the Delaware River not far from the artificial island that is home to the power company's Salem and Hope Creek generating stations.

Question: How do you know you're near a nuclear power plant? The cooling tower is the giveaway, if you're facing the right direction. Otherwise, it's those orange and black signs you encounter throughout the area, advising residents what to do should they (God forbid) hear the emergency sirens.

View of the Salem Generating Plant

Don't let these signs distract you from enjoying your trip. In fact, we have PSE&G to thank for instituting its wetlands program, intended to mitigate the future impact of the stations on fish life throughout the Delaware Bay area.

TRIVIA

There are two benches located at the parking area at the Fort Elfsborg Road entrance. One is dedicated to the crews of the *S.S. Phoenix* and *S.S. Pan Massachusetts*, who were killed in a collision on June 5, 1953. The other is dedicated to those who have lost their lives in the estuary.

52

Finn's Point Rear Range Light
"Born" in Buffalo

OVERVIEW

The Finn's Point Rear Range Light once played a vital role in New Jersey's southwest maritime history. Today the black-steel structure, more beautiful in an industrial rather than an aesthetic sense, is part of the Supawna Meadows National Wildlife Refuge. Visit this curiosity before or after visiting Finn's Point National Cemetery [see #53] and Fort Mott State Park [see #54].

HISTORY

Built for $1,200 in 1876 by the Kellogg Bridge Company for the U.S. Lighthouse Establishment, the 115-foot-tall light guided ships to their proper shipping lanes while they moved between the Delaware Bay and Delaware River.

The lighthouse keepers were presumably in good shape, since they had to tackle the 130-step trek up and down the light twice daily to light and extinguish the kerosene lamp. Keepers finally got a breather when the light was automated in 1934.

The light was dimmed for good in 1950, after the U.S. Army Corps of Engineers dredged the river channel. In the 1970s the state and a local citizen's

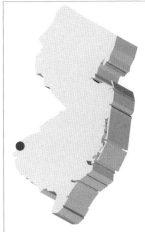

Finn's Point Rear Range Light
197 Lighthouse Road
Pennsville, NJ 08070 (Mailing Address)
Salem County
Phone: (856) 935-1487

Hours: The lighthouse is open from noon to 4 P.M. on the third Sunday of the month from April through October.
Fees: None
Facilities: Interpretive exhibits outside the lighthouse

Directions:
From the North: Take the New Jersey Turnpike south to Exit 1, and turn right at the Deepwater Ramp. Drive over the Route 295 overpass and turn left on Route 130. Follow Route 130 through Pennsville to Route 49 south. Turn right onto Route 630 (Fort Mott Road) and follow signs to the intersection of Routes 630 and 632, where the light is located.

From the South: Follow Route 49 north above Salem to Route 632 and follow signs.

group joined forces to restore the vandalized and deteriorating structure for historic purposes. It was placed on the National Register of Historic Places in 1983.

TRIVIA

According to the New Jersey Lighthouse Society, the light was built in Buffalo, New York, then transported to its location by train and mule wagon.

Finn's Point Rear Range Light as seen from Lighthouse Road

53

Finn's Point National Cemetery
Where Soldiers Sleep

OVERVIEW

I don't know whether I went on the best day or the worst to visit Finn's Point National Cemetery. It was early morning in the dead of winter, and the graves were buried under a heavy shroud of snow. Here and there were scattered little wreaths, with notes bearing thoughts from warmer, southerly states, like Alabama and the Carolinas.

Dressed in layers of polar fleece and goose down, I wondered if some of the dead would have preferred to be buried where they had lived, long before they ever heard of towns like Sharpsburg, Gettysburg, or Manassas. Still, there was beauty here. Perched in the grove overlooking the Delaware, surrounded by woods, it was a picturesque resting place.

Combine a visit to this somber but serene site with the adjoining Fort Mott State Park [see #54].

HISTORY

Finn's Point National Cemetery is home to the souls of 2,436 Confederate prisoners of war. Most had been captured during the three-day Battle of Gettysburg in July 1863, and interned at Fort Delaware on neighboring Pea

Finn's Point National Cemetery
Fort Mott Road
Pennsville, Salem County
Phone: (609) 877-5460
Web site: www.njparksandforests.org

Hours: Open daily from 8 A.M. to 5 P.M.
Fees: None
Facilities: Interpretive exhibits

Directions:
From the North: Take the New Jersey Turnpike south to Exit 1 and take the Deepwater ramp. Turn right at the end of the ramp, proceed over the Route 295 overpass, and turn left onto Route 130. This road will turn into Route 49. Continue through Pennsville to Route 630 (Fort Mott Road), and follow signs to the park. On the way, you'll pass Finn's Point Rear Range Light [see #52].

From the South: Follow Route 49 north through Salem to Route 630 and follow signs.

Patch Island. Their Union soldier guards are also buried here, and there are memorials to both.

The cemetery was originally part of Fort Mott. Together they comprised part of the Finn's Point Reservation, purchased by the U.S. government in the late 1830s. The cemetery was separated from the fort in 1943.

Monument to the Confederate dead at Finn's Point National Cementery ➤

54

Fort Mott State Park
End of the Trail—or the Beginning

OVERVIEW

Six miles south of the Delaware Memorial Bridge, Fort Mott State Park is considered the southern "anchor" of the Coastal Heritage Trail. Whether starting or ending your trip here, the fort is a great place for picnicking, hiking, and spending quality time with a little-known piece of New Jersey history.

Combine your visit here with one to adjoining Finn's Point National Cemetery [see #53].

HISTORY

Fort Mott was one of three coastal posts built in the 1870s to defend Delaware River ports, including Philadelphia; the other two were Fort Delaware on Pea Patch Island and Fort DuPont in Delaware City, Delaware.

Initially named the Battery at Finn's Point, the fort was renamed in 1897 in honor of Major General Gershom Mott (1822–1884), a Bordentown native who served in the Mexican-American and Civil wars, and was commander of the New Jersey National Guard.

Fort Mott State Park
104 acres
454 Fort Mott Road
Pennsville, NJ 08079
Salem County
Phone: (856) 935-3218
Web site: www.njparksandforests.org

Hours: Grounds open daily 8 A.M. to 7:30 P.M. Memorial Day through Labor Day; 8 A.M. to 4 P.M. remainder of the year

Fees: None

Facilities: Guided and self-guided walking tours; films, videos; picnic area, playground nature trail; ferry service to Fort Delaware, Pea Patch Island, Delaware available April through October

Directions:

From the North: Take the New Jersey Turnpike south to Exit 1 and take the Deepwater ramp. Turn right at the end of the ramp, proceed over the Route 295 overpass, and turn left onto Route 130. This road will turn into Route 49. Continue through Pennsville to Route 630 (Fort Mott Road), and follow signs to the park. You'll pass Finn's Point Rear Range Light [see #52] and Finn's Point National Cemetery [see #53] along the way.

From the South: Follow Route 49 north through Salem to Route 630 and follow signs to the park.

Battery at Fort Mott State Park

Like Sandy Hook's Fort Hancock [see #7], Fort Mott was a self-contained post, with 30 buildings, which included barracks, a hospital, post-exchange, school, and YMCA. Troops were stationed here between 1897 and 1922.

The guns were dismantled in 1943 and the fort was declared surplus. The state purchased the fort in 1947 as a historic site. It opened as Fort Mott State Park in 1951.

TRAILS

The guns are gone, but visitors can still prowl the grounds, including the top of the 750-foot-long parapet, a 35-foot-thick embankment of concrete and dirt; the fort's moat; and parados, a large, sloping mound used for defending the back side of the fort.

Observation tower ➤

A self-guided walking tour of the 104-acre property takes visitors along the fort's batteries, "disappearing" gun carriages, the plotting room used to calculate target ranges and locations, the fort's 52-foot fire control tower, and post headquarters.

A half-mile nature trail connects the fort with the adjacent Finn's Point National Historic Cemetery.

Fort Mott and Finn's Point National Cemetery were once part of the Finn's Point Reservation, bought by the U.S. in the late 1830s. The cemetery was separated from the fort in 1943.

TRIVIA

"Parados" is Spanish for "rear door." The word takes on a double meaning, since the fort's latrines were built into the parados.

Appendix A
Things to Do on the
New Jersey Coastal Heritage Trail

Here are specific activities you can enjoy on the New Jersey Coastal Heritage Trail. Items are listed according to region.

Bird-Watching

Sandy Hook Region

Perth Amboy Harbor Walk [#1]
Sandy Hook Unit of the Gateway National Recreation Area [#7]
Cheesequake State Park [#8]
Allaire State Park [#9]

Barnegat Bay Region

Cattus Island County Park [#10]
Island Beach State Park [#12]
Double Trouble State Park [#13]
Eno's Pond County Park [#15]
Barnegat Lighthouse State Park [#16]
Tuckerton Seaport [#18]
Great Bay Boulevard Wildlife Management Area [#19]

Absecon and Cape May Regions

Edwin B. Forsythe National Wildlife Refuge [#20]

Tuckahoe Wildlife Management Area [#23]
Corson's Inlet State Park [#24]
The Wetlands Institute [#25]
Cape May Migratory Bird Refuge [#27]
Cape May Point State Park [#28]
Higbee Beach Wildlife Management Area [#29]

Delsea Region

Cape May National Wildlife Refuge [#30]
Cape May Bird Observatory [#31]
Dennis Creek Wildlife Management Area [#32]
Belleplain State Forest [#33]
Eldora Nature Preserve [#34]
Dennis Township Wetland Restoration Site [#35]
Maurice River Township Wetland Restoration Site [#36]
East Point Lighthouse [#37]
Heislerville Wildlife Management Area [#38]
Commercial Township Wetland Restoration Site [#40]
Egg Island Wildlife Management Area [#41]
Glades Wildlife Refuge [#42]
Peaslee Wildlife Management Area [#44]
Manumuskin River Preserve [#45]
Peek Preserve [#46]
Green Swamp Nature Area [#47]
Stow Creek Viewing Area [#49]
Alloway Creek Watershed Wetland Restoration Site [#51]

Bicycling

Sandy Hook Region

Sandy Hook Unit of the Gateway National Recreation Area [#7]
Cheesequake State Park [#8]
Allaire State Park [#9]

Barnegat Bay Region

Cattus Island County Park [#10]
Island Beach State Park [#12]
Great Bay Boulevard Wildlife Management Area [#19]

Absecon and Cape May Regions
Edwin B. Forsythe National Wildlife Refuge [#20]

Delsea Region
Belleplain State Forest [#33]

Boating

Sandy Hook Region
Leonardo State Marina [#4]

Barnegat Bay Region
Island Beach State Park [#12]
Forked River State Marina [#14]
Great Bay Boulevard Wildlife Management Area [#19]

Absecon and Cape May Regions
Sen. Frank S. Farley State Marina [#22]
Tuckahoe Wildlife Management Area [#23]
Corson's Inlet State Park [#24]

Delsea Region
Dennis Creek Wildlife Management Area [#32]
Belleplain State Forest [#33]
Fortescue State Marina [#43]
Green Swamp Nature Area [#47]

Butterfly Watching

Sandy Hook Region
Sandy Hook Unit of the Gateway National Recreation Area [#7]
Cheesequake State Park [#8]
Allaire State Park [#9]

Barnegat Bay Region

Cattus Island County Park [#10]
Island Beach State Park [#12]
Eno's Pond County Park [#15]
Barnegat Lighthouse State Park [#16]
Tuckerton Seaport [#18]

Absecon and Cape May Regions

Edwin B. Forsythe National Wildlife Refuge [#20]
Corson's Inlet State Park [#24]
The Wetlands Institute [#25]
Hereford Inlet Lighthouse [#26]
Cape May Migratory Bird Refuge [#27]
Cape May Point State Park [#28]
Higbee Beach Wildlife Management Area [#29]

Delsea Region

Cape May National Wildlife Refuge [#30]
Cape May Bird Observatory [#31]
Belleplain State Forest [#33]
Eldora Nature Preserve [#34]
Green Swamp Nature Area [#47]

Camping

Sandy Hook Region

Cheesequake State Park [#8]
Allaire State Park [#9]

Delsea Region

Belleplain State Forest [#33]

Crabbing
Sandy Hook Region
Cheesequake State Park [#8]

Barnegat Bay Region
Island Beach State Park [#12]

Absecon and Cape May Regions
Corson's Inlet State Park [#24]

Delsea Region
Egg Island Wildlife Management Area [#41]

Cross-Country Skiing
Sandy Hook Region
Allaire State Park [#9]

Delsea Region
Belleplain State Forest [#33]

Dining
Sandy Hook Region
Perth Amboy Harbor Walk [#1]
Sandy Hook Unit of the Gateway National Recreation Area [#7]

Barnegat Bay Region
Tuckerton Seaport [#18]

Fishing
Sandy Hook Region
Sandy Hook Unit of the Gateway National Recreation Area [#7]
Cheesequake State Park [#8]

Barnegat Bay Region

Island Beach State Park [#12]
Barnegat Lighthouse State Park [#16]
Great Bay Boulevard Wildlife Management Area [#19]

Absecon and Cape May Regions

Corson's Inlet State Park [#24]
Cape May Point State Park [#28]

Delsea Region

Heislerville Wildlife Management Area [#38]

Hiking/Walking

Sandy Hook Region

Perth Amboy Harbor Walk [#1]
Mount Mitchill Scenic Overlook [#5]
Sandy Hook Unit of the Gateway National Recreation Area [#7]
Cheesequake State Park [#8]
Allaire State Park [#9]

Barnegat Bay Region

Cattus Island County Park [#10]
Island Beach State Park [#12]
Double Trouble State Park [#13]
Eno's Pond County Park [#15]
Barnegat Lighthouse State Park [#16]
Tuckerton Seaport [#18]
Great Bay Boulevard Wildlife Management Area [#19]

Absecon and Cape May Regions

Edwin B. Forsythe National Wildlife Refuge [#20]
Tuckahoe Wildlife Management Area [#23]

Corson's Inlet State Park [#24]
The Wetlands Institute [#25]
Cape May Migratory Bird Refuge [#27]
Cape May Point State Park [#28]
Higbee Beach Wildlife Management Area [#29]

Delsea Region

Cape May National Wildlife Refuge [#30]
Cape May Bird Observatory [#31]
Dennis Creek Wildlife Management Area [#32]
Belleplain State Forest [#33]
Eldora Nature Preserve [#34]
Dennis Township Wetland Restoration Site [#35]
Maurice River Township Wetland Restoration Site [#36]
Heislerville Wildlife Management Area [#38]
Commercial Township Wetland Restoration Site [#40]
Egg Island Wildlife Management Area [#41]
Glades Wildlife Refuge [#42]
Peaslee Wildlife Management Area [#44]
Manumuskin River Preserve [#45]
Peek Preserve [#46]
Green Swamp Nature Area [#47]
Stow Creek Viewing Area [#49]
Alloway Creek Watershed Wetland Restoration Site [#51]
Fort Mott State Park [#54]

History and Coastal Heritage

Sandy Hook Region

Perth Amboy Harbor Walk [#1]
Steamboat Dock Museum [#2]
Twin Lights State Historic Site [#6]
Sandy Hook Unit of the Gateway National Recreation Area [#7]
Allaire State Park [#9]

Barnegat Bay Region

Toms River Seaport Society Maritime Museum [#11]
Double Trouble State Park [#13]
Barnegat Lighthouse State Park [#16]
U.S. Coast Guard Station, Barnegat Light [#17]
Tuckerton Seaport [#18]

Absecon and Cape May Regions

U.S. Coast Guard Station, Atlantic City [#21]
The Wetlands Institute [#25]
Hereford Inlet Lighthouse [#26]
Cape May Point State Park [#28]

Delsea Region

East Point Lighthouse [#37]
Bayshore Discovery Project [#39]
Fortescue State Marina [#43]
Greenwich Tea Burning Monument [#48]
Hancock House State Historic Site [#50]
Finn's Point Rear Range Light [#52]
Finn's Point National Cemetery [#53]
Fort Mott State Park [#54]

Hunting

Note: You must have the appropriate state and local hunting, firearm, and bow-hunting licenses to hunt in any of these locations. For more information, or if you would like to learn more about hunting, call the New Jersey Division of Fish and Wildlife at (856) 629-0090.

Barnegat Bay Region

Great Bay Boulevard Wildlife Management Area [#19]

Absecon and Cape May Regions

Edwin B. Forsythe National Wildlife Refuge [#20]
Tuckahoe Wildlife Management Area [#23]
Higbee Beach Wildlife Management Area [#29]

Delsea Region

Dennis Creek Wildlife Management Area [#32]
Heislerville Wildlife Management Area [#38]
Peaslee Wildlife Management Area [#44]
Alloway Creek Watershed Wetland Restoration Site [#51]

Lighthouses

Sandy Hook Region

Twin Lights State Historic Site [#6]
Sandy Hook Unit of the Gateway National Recreation Area [#7]

Barnegat Bay Region

Barnegat Lighthouse State Park [#16]
Tuckerton Seaport [#18]

Absecon and Cape May Regions

Hereford Inlet Lighthouse [#26]
Cape May Point State Park [#28]

Delsea Region

East Point Lighthouse [#37]
Finn's Point Rear Range Light [#52]

Paddling

Sandy Hook Region

Sandy Hook Unit of the Gateway National Recreation Area [#7]
Cheesequake State Park [#8]

Barnegat Bay Region

Island Beach State Park [#12]
Great Bay Boulevard Wildlife Management Area [#19]

Photography

Sen. Frank S. Farley State Marina [#22]
Tuckahoe Wildlife Management Area [#23]
Corson's Inlet State Park [#24]
The Wetlands Institute [#25]
Hereford Inlet Lighthouse [#26]
Cape May Migratory Bird Refuge [#27]
Cape May Point State Park [#28]
Higbee Beach Wildlife Management Area [#29]

Delsea Region

Cape May National Wildlife Refuge [#30]
Cape May Bird Observatory [#31]
Dennis Creek Wildlife Management Area [#32]
Belleplain State Forest [#33]
Eldora Nature Preserve [#34]
Dennis Township Wetland Restoration Site [#35]
Maurice River Township Wetland Restoration Site [#36]
East Point Lighthouse [#37]
Heislerville Wildlife Management Area [#38]
Bayshore Discovery Project [#39]
Commercial Township Wetland Restoration Site [#40]
Egg Island Wildlife Management Area [#41]
Glades Wildlife Refuge [#42]
Forstecue State Marina [#43]
Peaslee Wildlife Management Area [#44]
Manumuskin River Preserve [#45]
Peek Preserve [#46]
Green Swamp Nature Area [#47]
Stow Creek Viewing Area [#49]
Hancock House State Historic Site [#50]
Alloway Creek Watershed Wetland Restoration Site [#51]
Finn's Point National Cemetery [#53]
Fort Mott State Park [#54]

Picnic Areas

Sandy Hook Region
Sandy Hook Unit of the Gateway National Recreation Area [#7]
Cheesequake State Park [#8]
Allaire State Park [#9]

Barnegat Bay Region
Island Beach State Park [#12]
Double Trouble State Park [#13]
Eno's Pond County Park [#15]
Barnegat Lighthouse State Park [#16]

Absecon and Cape May Regions
Edwin B. Forsythe National Wildlife Refuge [#20]
Cape May Point State Park [#28]

Delsea Region
Belleplain State Forest [#33]
Fort Mott State Park [#54]

Swimming and Sunbathing

Sandy Hook Region
Sandy Hook Unit of the Gateway National Recreation Area [#7]
Cheesequake State Park [#8]

Barnegat Bay Region
Island Beach State Park [#12]
Barnegat Lighthouse State Park (Sunbathing only) [#16]

Absecon and Cape May Regions
Corson's Inlet State Park (Sunbathing only) [#24]
Cape May Point State Park (Sunbathing only) [#28]

Delsea Region
Belleplain State Forest [#33]

Windsurfing

Sandy Hook Region
Sandy Hook Unit of the Gateway National Recreation Area [#7]

Barnegat Bay Region
Island Beach State Park [#12]

Appendix B
Recommended Reading

Boyd, Howard P. 1991. *A Field Guide to the Pine Barrens of New Jersey: Its Flora, Fauna, Ecology and Historic Sites.* Medford, NJ: Plexus Publishing, Inc.

Boyd, Howard P. 1997. *A Pine Barrens Odyssey: A Naturalist's Year in the Pine Barrens.* Medford, NJ: Plexus Publishing, Inc.

Boyd, Howard P. 2001. *Wildflowers of the Pine Barrens of New Jersey.* Medford, NJ: Plexus Publishing, Inc.

Boyle, William J., Jr. 2002. *A Guide to Bird Finding in New Jersey.* New Brunswick, NJ: Rutgers University Press.

Collins, Beryl Robichaud, and Karl Anderson. 1994. *Plant Communities of New Jersey: A Study in Landscape Diversity.* New Brunswick, NJ: Rutgers University Press.

Davis, Millard. 1997. *Natural Pathways of New Jersey: A Look at 100 of New Jersey's Finest Natural Places.* Medford, NJ: Plexus Publishing, Inc.

Johnson, Libbie Harrover. 1997. *One Hundred Years and Still Counting.* Bernardsville, NJ: New Jersey Audubon Society.

Murray, Steve. 2001. *A Guide to the Hereford Inlet Lighthouse Gardens: With Tips and Observations for the Seashore Gardener.* North Wildwood, NJ: Hereford Inlet Lighthouse Commission.

Peterson, Robert A. 1998. *Patriots, Pirates, and Pineys: Sixty Who Shaped New Jersey.* Medford, NJ: Plexus Publishing, Inc.

Peterson, Robert A. 2005. *Natural Wonders of the Jersey Pines and Shore.* Medford, NJ: Plexus Publishing, Inc.

Robinson, Patricia. 2003. *Wonderwalks: The Trails of New Jersey Audubon.* Medford, NJ: Plexus Publishing, Inc.

Sibley, David. 1987. *The Birds of Cape May.* Bernardsville, NJ: New Jersey Audubon Society.

Solem-Stull, Barbara. 2005. *Ghost Towns and Other Quirky Places in the New Jersey Pine Barrens.* Medford, NJ: Plexus Publishing, Inc.

Walsh, Joan, Vince Elia, Richard Kane, and Thomas Haliwell. 1999. *Birds of New Jersey.* Bernardsville, NJ: New Jersey Audubon Society.

Appendix C
Recommended Web Sites

For general information on the New Jersey Coastal Heritage Trail, consult the Web site run by the New Jersey Department of Environmental Protection, www.state.nj.us/dep/parksandforests. Information on PSE&G's Estuary Enhancement Program can be obtained by visiting www.pseg.com and clicking on "environment."

Additionally, various groups involved with specific sites along the trail offer the following Web sites, which generally include historical information, fees, schedules of events, and directions.

Bayshore Discovery Project/*A. J. Meerwald*, www.bayshorediscoveryproject.org
    or www.ajmeerwald.org

Cape May Bird Observatory, www.njaudubon.org

Information on the Sandy Hook Bird Observatory, in the Fort Hancock Historic District of the Sandy Hook Gateway National Recreation Area, may also be obtained at the New Jersey Audubon site.

Cape May Point State Park, www.njparksandforests.org

Edwin B. Forsythe National Wildlife Refuge, http://forsythe.fws.gov

Eno's Pond County Park, www.co.ocean.nj.us

Hereford Inlet Lighthouse, www.herefordlighthouse.org

Island Beach State Park

> Those interested in fishing at the park should visit the Web site of the Jersey Coast Anglers Association, www.jcaa.org; information on the use of all-terrain vehicles can be obtained at the Web site of the New Jersey Beach Buggy Association, www.njbba.org; Save Barnegat Bay is a nonprofit environmental group located at www.savebarnegatbay.org; another nonprofit, Friends of Island Beach, can be found at www.friendsofisland beach.com

Toms River Seaport Museum, www.tomsriverseaport.com

Tuckerton Seaport Museum, www.tuckertonseaport.org

Twin Lights State Historic Site, www.twin-lights.org

Wetlands Institute, www.wetlandsinstitute.org

For more information on books published by Plexus Publishing, go to www.plexuspublishing.com.

About the Author

Born in Paterson, New Jersey, Patricia Robinson is a lifelong resident of the Garden State. She has been a freelance travel writer, a public relations executive, a trade magazine editor, and, most recently, an award-winning reporter/photographer for a chain of award-winning weekly newspapers in Central Jersey. She is the author of *Wonderwalks: The Trails of New Jersey Audubon* (2003, Plexus Publishing, Inc.).

Index

C